BRING IN THE SPRING

Sarah is severely physically disabled. She has no way of communicating with the outside world and is angry and frustrated about what life has offered her.

Bel is a teenage school girl experiencing all the problems and insecurities that come with her age.

When Bel starts a community project at Willowbank School where Sarah goes, an enriching experience begins for both of them. They each embark on a journey of discovery, revealing strengths they never knew they had.

ABOUT THE AUTHOR

Hannah Cole read psychology at King's College, Cambridge and later taught disadvantaged adults. She now lives in Headington, Oxford with her family of three children. She has written a number of children's books, this being her third full-length novel.

HANNAH COLE

Bring in the Spring

HEINEMANN
NEW WINDMILLS

For Kerry

Heinemann Educational
a division of
Heinemann Publishers (Oxford) Ltd
Halley Court, Jordan Hill, Oxford OX2 8EJ
OXFORD LONDON EDINBURGH
MADRID ATHENS BOLOGNA PARIS
MELBOURNE SYDNEY AUCKLAND SINGAPORE TOKYO
IBADAN NAIROBI HARARE GABORONE
PORTSMOUTH NH (USA)

First published in Great Britain by Julia MacRae, an imprint of Random House

First published in the New Windmill Series 1994

95 96 97 98 10 9 8 7 6 5 4 3 2

ISBN 0 435 12421 8

British Library Cataloguing in Publication Data
for this title is available from the British Library

Cover illustration by John Slater

Typeset by CentraCet Limited, Cambridge
Printed and bound in England by Clays Ltd, St Ives plc

1 Snowdrop House

The other children were down on the lawn. They were all excited about being allowed on the new play house. Most of it had been standing there for months, but only this week had the last bolts been fastened, and the fence taken away from round it. Sylvia was already up on its roof. She was always climbing on things. Today Mrs Eaton and Davina were letting her climb because the play house was surrounded by black rubber tiles, so she would not be badly hurt if she did fall down. Joe was walking slowly round, taking little steps, softly touching the different parts of the house: the rough bark of the log walls, the smooth shiny heads of the bolts that held them together. Duncan had settled into the house and Sarah could hear him inviting people in for cups of tea. With everyone out of doors it felt almost like summer again, except that they were wearing their coats and hats, and Joe had his scarf wound twice round his neck and tied under his chin.

Sarah looked at the pattern of light wood and dark wood and the moving patterns of children being busy, up and down, in and out, or gentle touch touch touch as Joe inspected the building. The sun had nearly reached the band of blue sky above the trees. It was about to come out below the cloud that was hiding it. Down it came, emerging from the cloud like an upside-down sunrise, and the garden became golden. Even the hard earth in the flower-beds had little golden peaks among the lumps of shadow. It was ages since the Council gardeners had come to take out the dead flowers. Sarah hoped it would not be long before they arrived with new ones for the spring. She liked to be there to watch them.

"We'll have to keep a close eye on them for the first week or so," Mrs Eaton said to Davina, over Sarah's head. Sarah was used to listening to things said above her head, or behind her, but Mrs Eaton so often said the same things that it was hardly worth listening. "It's always the same with new equipment. One of the children will think of some ridiculous way of half killing themselves or someone else. When the novelty has worn off they will settle down." Mrs Eaton did not like the children unsettled. It made for hard work.

Sarah looked up at Davina, who was standing beside her buggy. Davina's long hair was hanging down, and Sarah could not see her face.

"It's a shame they didn't finish putting it up in the summer," said Davina. "You don't get many nice days like this, this time of year. Shall I take Sarah over and let her have a look?"

"Oh, I shouldn't bother," said Mrs Eaton, on Sarah's other side. "It's so difficult pushing this thing over the rough grass, and she's better off up here, out of the noise. She wouldn't know what it was all about. Look, she's kicking her legs again. I wonder if we should strap them down? I wouldn't like her to hurt herself." She pushed the buggy to and fro a few times, which made Sarah's head jolt.

"She's getting heavy, isn't she?" said Davina.

"You should have seen her when we first had her," said Mrs Eaton. "You weren't working here then, but she was a scrawny little baby. Pathetic. Now I put off getting her up in the morning, it's such a strain lugging her around to get her clothes on."

"Well, it doesn't make a lot of difference to her

2

whether you get her up or not," said Davina. "It's sad really, isn't it?"

"I think it's ever so good of her mother to keep in touch," said Mrs Eaton, "with Sarah the way she is."

"She doesn't have any other children, does she?"

"No," said Mrs Eaton. "She lives on her own. It must have been a tragedy for her, having Sarah. She's quite an intelligent woman."

Sarah kicked again. If only she could move the buggy, roll it down to the grass where the other children were playing. She wanted to know what was inside the house, and what Duncan was doing in there.

"She's thrashing around again," said Davina.

"Overexcited," said Mrs Eaton. "Better take her indoors to the quiet room. She's nearly due for her medicine anyway."

"That reminds me," Davina said. "I've got to get to the chemist before it shuts to fetch those ear drops for Duncan. I'll give Sarah her medicine and wheel her down with me. She always quietens down when she's moving along. Do you want me to take any of the others with me? I could manage a couple of quiet ones."

"No, it's all right," said Mrs Eaton. "They're all happy out here. Get me some shampoo while you're there, will you?"

"You could use the stuff from the kids' bathroom," said Davina.

"Oh, I don't like that cheap stuff," said Mrs Eaton. "I have the herbal sort, for frequent use. I'll pay you back at lunch-time."

I don't like the cheap stuff either, said Sarah. It smells of mouldy apples.

"I'd best be off," said Davina. "Before she gets really noisy. See you later."

Sarah was tipped back in the chair and spun round,

3

and they set off down the drive. She was always afraid that Davina would let go of her while she closed the gate after them, and she would roll down the sloping pavement into the road. It hadn't happened yet.

"Off to the chemist, then, Sarah," said Davina. "Shall we go through the park and see if there's any conkers left?"

All the children had collected conkers in the autumn, and Snowdrop House was still full of them, small and shrivelled now. Duncan had hundreds in his locker. Sarah did not know what they saw in them. But she liked the park, even now that the trees had lost all their leaves. It was good to see things that had not been planned by Mrs Eaton and the other grown-ups, leaves flying around, dogs chasing each other, squirrels scampering along branches.

"It still gets dark really early, doesn't it?" said Davina. "I hate it. Roll on the spring." Sarah knew that she was really talking to herself, but she preferred that to being pushed along in silence, which sometimes happened.

They passed the playground. A mother was pushing her child in the swing, keeping one hand warm in her coat pocket. The child kicked its feet and one of its boots fell off. Then Davina had pushed Sarah past, and the child and its mother were out of sight. Sarah imagined the mother stopping the swing, bending to pick the boot up, and pushing it back on to the child's foot. But it could be that the mother did not notice, and the child had to hobble home in only one boot. Or a squirrel could have crept out, snatched the boot and scampered off up a tree with it. Or the mother could have bent down and been knocked out by the swing, and now be lying there unconscious. Sarah ran out of ideas and relaxed in the buggy.

Two girls walked towards them along the path, talking loudly. "The playgroup would be a lot better,"

4

the shorter one was saying. "You'll never get a chance like that again."

"You can if you want," the other girl said. She was tall and thin with long black hair coming out under her woolly hat. "I want to know what that sort of school is like."

"I don't," answered her friend. "It gives me the creeps thinking about it."

The tall girl nudged her and nodded towards Sarah. They giggled, then straightened their faces and said nothing until they had gone past Sarah and were out of sight behind. She heard the conversation start again, quieter and with more giggles.

Now along came a boy, about Sarah's age. He was swaying from side to side, looking up into the bare branches of a tree and muttering to himself. "Sixty-four times twenty-four, that's sixty-four hundred divided by four, one thousand six hundred, take away sixty-four."

Sarah wondered what sort of counting that was. She only knew about one, two, three, four.

"Peculiar little boy," said Davina. "Talking to himself." She sniffed, and rattled the buggy over the gravel at the park entrance. They swung round towards the chemist's.

2   Bell and Claire

"The playgroup would be a lot better," said Bel, kicking a wrinkled old conker along the path. "You'll never get a chance like that again."

"You can if you want," said Claire. "I want to know what that sort of school is like."

"I don't," said Bel. "It gives me the creeps thinking about it." She thought about handicapped children. Would they dribble? How could you play with children who didn't understand what you said to them?

Claire nudged her. There was a handicapped child coming towards them, in a wheel-chair. A giant push-chair really. She looked weird, poor little thing. Such thin legs in tight red trousers, and her head all sideways leaning against the striped canvas back of the chair. Her eyes met Bel's, but they probably didn't see anything. How embarrassing that Bel had been talking about handicapped children. Bel looked sideways at Claire. She was pretending to be serious, but she let half a giggle out of the side of her mouth. Bel burst out laughing, and tried to think of a good excuse.

"What do you call a crocodile on a tennis court?"

The wheelchair came up to them and passed them. Bel looked back at it. It had small wheels. It looked hard work pushing it over the bumps in the path.

"Paul's miles behind," she said. "Shall we wait for him?" Paul was Claire's younger brother.

"He'll catch up," said Claire. "He'll run when he notices we've got ahead. So what do you call a crocodile on a tennis court?"

"I don't know," said Bel. "I just made it up, to have an excuse for giggling. It was a bit embarrassing. I just didn't notice her. But don't you see what I mean? Children like that one. What can you say to them? What could we do with them?"

"Willowbank isn't for physically handicapped children," said Claire. "It's children with learning difficulties, so they'll just be like younger children, say, toddlers. You like babies, don't you?"

"Little babies," said Bel.

"Anyway, Miss Radcot said it's their activities afternoon, when we'd be there. We'd just be helping with painting, or taking them for walks, or baking cakes. The teachers will tell us what to do."

Bel knew that she would not win the argument, but she had a last try. "But if we don't do the playgroup building, that stupid Dylan will do it with some of his friends, and he'll make a mess of it, with Superman all over the outside or something. We could do it really well, and you know you could do pictures that the children would love."

"They'll probably love Superman," said Claire. "I would quite like to do it, but I'd rather do Willowbank. I saw this really good programme on the telly about grown-ups with learning difficulties. Some of them can be quite independent, and lead lives of their own. It depends how they're treated, and if they're encouraged to do things for themselves."

"Well, we're not going to make any difference to people's lives, going one afternoon a week," Bel objected.

"Especially if we're just doing what the teachers tell us to do."

"You never know," said Claire. "We might make a

difference. Anyway, I want to find out more about it. Might help me understand Paul, anyway."

Bel looked at her enquiringly.

"He's got learning difficulties," said Claire. "You can never find anything for him to learn. He knows it all already."

They waited at the park gate for Paul to catch up.

"I don't see the point of these community projects anyway," said Bel. "It's just an excuse for Miss Radcot to get rid of us for the afternoon."

"It might be good," said Claire. "Make a change from school. Come on, slow-coach!" she shouted to Paul. "What were you staring at all the trees for?"

"I've been working out how many leaves there are here in the summer," said Paul. "I thought about it in August, but it was harder to count the branches then. These big sycamores have an average of two point three eight main trunks, and each of those has about ten big branches off it, and the big branches have about twelve sub-branches . . ."

"So how many are there altogether?" Bel asked quickly. She could feel Claire next to her getting irritated.

"I think about seven million on all the trees in the park," Paul said, "not counting the bushes. But that's only a very rough estimate. It's amazing that so many leaves can just rot away, isn't it?"

"They don't just rot away, stupid," said Claire. "The gardeners come and take trailer-loads away. If they didn't we'd be wading through mouldy leaves and all the grass would be dead."

"Well, they take them away to a Council compost heap somewhere," said Paul. "Then they rot away and get put back on the flowerbeds, don't they?"

"If you don't walk a bit faster," said Claire, "you'll rot away. And the skating session will be over before we get there."

Bel felt a little guilty about Paul. She was the outsider on these Saturday afternoons with Claire and Paul's father. Maybe if she were not here, Paul would not be so obviously the odd one out. But Claire always wanted her to come, and their father seemed to welcome her, and besides, it was good to get a free trip to the ice rink, or the bowling alley, or whatever their father had planned that Saturday. But Bel felt obliged to be kind to Paul. "Can you skate, Paul?"

"Yes."

Bel looked at him to see if there was more answer coming, but he obviously thought there was no more to be said.

"You needn't bother asking," said Claire, rather bitterly. "He's brilliant at it, of course. The first time Dad took us, Paul just watched. He wouldn't go on the ice until the session was nearly over. He said he was studying how the experts were doing it. And then he knew how to do it."

"I did fall over a lot," said Paul.

"Only because you were trying to twirl round on one foot," said Claire. "You could go along, forwards and backwards, and I was still clinging on to the sides. It's not fair. I hate little brothers."

"I suppose Gilly hates little sisters," said Bel.

Bel's sister seemed to hate most people at the moment. It was all Godfrey's fault, the boyfriend who had dumped Gilly. She should just keep her hating for him, and let everyone else be. But it was always like this when they split up. Until they got together again, the flat was going to be a gloomy place. When Miss Radcot, the social studies teacher at Bel's school, had told them about the community project that they would all be doing every Wednesday, the idea of helping to paint bright pictures on the ugly grey walls of the playgroup building across the road from school had appealed to Bel as an escape from thinking about

9

people and their dissatisfaction with each other. The special school that Claire had set her heart on visiting was likely to be full of dissatisfaction. Nobody could be very satisfied where handicapped people were concerned. It would all be anxiety and hard work.

"What are you frowning about?" said Claire. "You don't mind Paul being better on skates than us, do you? Or are you a secret ice skating star?"

Bel laughed. "I've only been once, and then Gilly hired me the wrong size boots, so I got terrible blisters. I'll probably spend the whole time sitting on the ice."

The domed roof of the ice rink was in sight now, and even Paul began to hurry.

"You don't mind me not doing the playgroup with you, do you?" Claire asked, as though it was an afterthought.

"I might as well come and do Willowbank with you," said Bel. "Dylan can do Superman. It's too cold for painting out of doors, anyway."

"There's Dad," said Paul, and ran towards him. The community project was settled.

3 Willowbank School

Most of the pupils at Willowbank Special School arrived in minibuses; only a few were brought in by their parents. Eleven children walked up each morning from Snowdrop House, holding hands two by two, except for Sylvia, who needed a grown-up of her own to keep her going in the right direction. The other grown-up pushed Sarah in her buggy. They were always early to school because the staff at Snowdrop House were in a hurry to get back to their morning chores.

"Good morning, Sarah," said Mrs Hinksey as Davina wheeled her into the classroom. "Good morning, Duncan. Good morning, Joe."

Duncan rushed in to hug Mrs Hinksey. "Good morning, Mrs Hinksey, good morning, Mrs Hinksey!"

"All right, Duncan, all right," said Mrs Hinksey calmly. "Go and hang up your things."

Joe was standing at Mrs Hinksey's elbow, biting his lip. "Mrs, Mrs, Mrs," he stuttered.

"What is it, Joe?"

"He's found something for you on the way here," said Davina. "He wouldn't show me what it was."

Mrs Hinksey looked into Joe's little hand. "Oh, what a lovely snail shell, Joe," she said. "Well done! Shall we put it on the nature table?"

Sarah let Davina take off her jacket and woolly hat. It was a stupid hat, white with fluff all round it. Her own hat had got lost, and this was a spare one. It was a relief to get it off.

"Shall I put her on the mat, Mrs Hinksey?" Davina asked.

"No, dear, it's all right," said Mrs Hinksey. "It will be assembly soon. She may as well stay in the buggy. I hope we're going to have no kicking today, Sarah."

Davina put the brake on the buggy and set off back to the house.

Mrs Hinksey encouraged Joe with his buttons and gave him a puzzle to put together. Duncan fetched one for himself.

"Now, Sarah," said Mrs Hinksey. "I've got some work for you to do before assembly." She pushed her up to one of the small tables and brought out a wooden stand with a stick fixed into it.

"Here are some rings, Sarah," she said. "One, two, three, four rings." Mrs Hinksey knew that the numbers meant nothing to Sarah, but there was not much one could do for Sarah except talk to her, and besides, David was standing at her elbow. In any case, she had been teaching children like these for so long that she sometimes found herself counting her buttons aloud as she fastened her own cardigan in the mornings. "Here's a red one, Sarah, like your nice red trousers. Here's a yellow one. This one is blue. Now, here is the green one." She waved it in front of Sarah's face. "I want you to put them on the stick. I know you can do it."

She put the red ring into Sarah's hand. At the first try, the whole stand slid across the table. Mrs Hinksey pulled it back and held it in place. The few quiet minutes before the minibuses arrived was usually the best time for Mrs Hinksey to spend with Sarah on her own. Sarah tried hard to finish the task so that she would be allowed to lie on the floor. The buggy was uncomfortable after a while. With huge concentration, she aimed the ring at the stick. To her surprise, her arm went in exactly the right direction, and the ring slid onto the stick.

"Good girl!" said Mrs Hinksey. "I knew you could do it! No, let go. Don't pull it off again. Here, try the next one. This one is blue. See, blue?" She put the blue ring into Sarah's hand and went to meet David, whose mother had just brought him in.

Sarah aimed the ring but her arm moved too suddenly and knocked the stand right off the table onto the floor. The red ring fell off. Sarah swept the other rings off the table as well.

David jumped up and down and hid his face in his elbow. "Naughty Sarah!" he squeaked. "Naughty Sarah!"

"Oh, what a pity, Sarah!" said Mrs Hinksey reprovingly. "I thought you were going to try your best for me today. Never mind, perhaps tomorrow." She picked up the rings, put them on the stand and tucked it away on the shelf.

The minibus children arrived and Sarah breathed a sigh of relief. Her education was over for the day. Perhaps after assembly she would be left alone.

"David will push Sarah," announced David firmly.

"Well, push carefully," said Mrs Hinksey. "No rushing. And take her over to the wheelchair corner."

There were three other children in the school who used wheelchairs, and they were all parked together at the back of the hall where they would not block anyone's view. There were some tiny children in the babies' class who could not walk either, but the helpers carried them into assembly.

"Look," whispered the girl parked next to Sarah. "Visitors."

There were often visitors at Willowbank School. Doctors and student teachers and speech therapists came to watch the classes, and sometimes the fat man from the pub came to decide what to raise money for next. He had collected for the play house at Snowdrop House, and now he was organising a sponsored fried-egg race to raise money for a special sort of round-about for the school playground.

Two of them, Sarah tried to whisper back. Not doctors.

"Can someone take Sarah out if she makes any more of those noises?" the headmistress called to the helpers at the back of the hall. "All right, then. Good morning, everyone!" There was a general roar, which was the school saying good morning back to the headmistress. "Well, it's another bright day today, and Mrs Wallace has brought in some lovely flowers to remind us that spring is on the way. Put up your hand if you can tell me what sort of flowers they are. Carmen?"

"I think, I think they are roses," said Carmen, with her hand still held staight up in the air.

"A good try, Carmen," said the headmistress, "but no, these are not roses. You can put your hand down now. Anyone else?"

Daffodils! Sarah shouted out. Everyone knows daffodils.

"I think you had better take Sarah out, please," said the headmistress. "It does make things difficult for the others. Nobody? Well, they are daffodils. I don't think we'll be getting daffodils in our gardens for a little while yet. I expect these were grown in a greenhouse. Now, I've heard that a little boy in Mrs Hinksey's class has been working very hard already this morning. What has Duncan done, Mrs Hinksey?"

While Mrs Hinksey led Duncan up to the front, holding a tray in her other hand, Sarah was wheeled out into the corridor and spun round so that she could still see into the hall.

"It is the first time that he has done this puzzle," Mrs Hinksey was saying, with her hand on Duncan's shoulder. "And he managed it all on his own."

14

"Well done, Duncan," said the headmistress. "A big clap for Duncan. Any other special news? Oh, yes, Katie's new glasses. They are smart, Katie. All right, sit down again. Now, Mrs Wallace will play for us and we will all sing 'He's got the whole world in his hands'. Let's all stand up."

Sarah waited for the song to finish. They sang it too slowly. Then the children were told to put their hands together, close their eyes, and say thank you for the sunshine and their lovely school. Sarah could see the other children's eyes obediently screwed up tight. She couldn't put her hands together. She felt bent and uncomfortable, and she was not thanking anyone for anything.

4 Willowbank School

Back in the classroom, Sarah lay on the carpet in the quiet corner. Mrs Hinksey had propped up a card against the wall directly in front of her eyes. She put it sideways, so that it was the right way round for Sarah to see the pictures on it. The picture was a farm, all green, and divided into six square fields. There was one bull in the first field, two cows in the second, three sheep, four pigs, five hens, six ducks. Mrs Hinksey did give her a different picture to look at each day, but Sarah knew this one by heart. She could close her eyes and still see it.

She ran through all the thoughts that she had had before about the farm. She had decided on the animals' characters. The bull looked shy and pleasant, and you could see that the pigs were mean. The ducks were nothing, just a noisy nuisance. Sarah had thought of different ways of arranging the animals. You could have one duck in each field, but the other animals wouldn't share out fairly. You could put the bull with the ducks, and it would be the same size family as if you put the cows with the hens, or the sheep with the pigs. But the cows had their noses in the air, and they might tread on the hens. Sarah imagined that Mrs Hinksey had put the card the other way round and quickly worked out which order the fields would have been in then. Or if it had been upside-down, which way then. Or facing the wall? It did not take long to solve that puzzle. Sarah could think of nothing else interesting about the farm. She waited for the day to crash and screech its way past her. She was turned over, moved, brought to the table for milk, sat on Mrs Hinksey's lap for the story, taken for dinner. After the dinner hour she was put back on the mat. She could not see what was going on in the classroom behind her back, but she could hear the scraping of chairs, and David going on and on about something, and Mrs Hinksey trying to persuade Sylvia to sit down and join in.

Suddenly David's voice rose higher, and Sarah heard him saying insistently, "Good morning, good morning, good morning," until a voice answered him. "Good afternoon, David. I've come to speak to Mrs Hinksey. You get on with your work."

It was Miss Wastie, the headteacher. Sarah listened, although the conversation was sure to be boring.

"Good afternoon, Mrs Hinksey," said Miss Wastie. "This is Isabel, our volunteer from St Francis' School, who will be coming here every Wednesday to help us with our activities. As this is the first week of term, Isabel, we are keeping the children in their own classrooms to let them settle down. You'll see next Wednesday what we get up to for our activities sessions. Then the children get grouped according to which activity they will benefit from most. Now, Mrs Hinksey, I've popped Isabel's friend Claire in with the tinies, and I've brought Isabel along to you, because I thought if they could just see what goes on in one of our classrooms, it would give them a better idea of what we are trying to do. Is that all right? I am sure that Mrs Hinksey will find something useful for you to do, Isabel."

"It's always useful to have an extra pair of hands," said Mrs Hinksey. "I expect Miss Wastie has told you what sort of children we cater for. We're mostly concerned with teaching skills for living, and of course modifying behaviour to make it easier for our children to fit into society. There is very little academic teaching as you would know it. But what may seem a small achievement to you may be quite a milestone to a child. Don't feel shy. You can ask about anything you want to know."

Sarah listened. Sylvia had to be rescued from the sink, where she was washing some books. Duncan had finished putting pegs into the pegboard, and tipped the board up by mistake. The visitor, Isabel, was asked to help him pick them up. Sarah could hear Mrs Hinksey saying that he didn't have to put the pegs in all over again; she was sure he had done it beautifully. But Duncan insisted that he would have to do it again. He sounded close to tears.

"I'd like you to get to know a few of the children on a one-to-one basis," Mrs Hinksey said. "Then you'll have a better idea of what to expect of them."

The visitor said nothing at all; at least Sarah did not hear her.

"I'm David Anthony Stimson," Sarah heard. "I'm David Anthony Stimson. How are you? What's your name?"

"My name is Bel – Isabel," said a rather quiet voice.

"My name is David Anthony Stimson," said David. "What's your name?"

"All right, David," said Mrs Hinksey, "Let me see you colour in those shapes. Maybe we'll start with Joe, Isabel. This is Joe. He's a very good boy, aren't you, Joe? And he loves to have some individual attention."

Sarah imagined Joe looking anxiously up into Mrs Hinksey's face. He would be biting his lip and nodding his head as though he could not stop.

"We'll settle you in the quiet corner, where you can sit together," said Mrs Hinksey. "And perhaps you

18

could look at a book with him and get him to talk about the pictures? He does have quite a few words of speech, but he doesn't use them very much. Now, what book would be best?"

They came over to the quiet corner and Mrs Hinksey rolled Sarah on to her other side to give her a different view. Joe was sitting stiffly next to the visitor on the bench against the wall, and looking round up into her face to see what she was expecting him to do. The visitor had a big picture book open on her lap and she was smiling shyly at Joe.

Sarah recognised her. She had seen that girl giggling in the park. In the park Sarah had thought she was silly. She wondered now what she was doing here. The girl's cheeks had been pink in the park, bright round pink cheeks from the cold, like the cheeks on children in pictures. Today her whole face, with its big pointed nose and little crinkly eyes, was pink. She must be embarrassed. She was bending, trying to get down to Joe's level. Her face was round. She was nearly as big as Mrs Hinksey. She was wearing those clothes that big children seemed to wear a lot of the time, a dark blue skirt and a dark blue cardigan and a white shirt. Sarah thought, "If I ever get to choose my clothes I won't ever wear dark blue or white. I'll wear orange and red and yellow and green, stripes and spots, rainbows all over." She did not think much of Bel, wearing those dull clothes, her odd face blushing pink, and bending down as though she was not sure that she should be there.

Bel opened the book at the first page. It was a book about school, with plenty of details in the large pictures.

"Look, Joe, what can you see in this picture?"

Joe tapped the page with his finger and smiled questioningly at Bel. Sarah could see that he wanted very much to please her. She did not know why the

19

children were so anxious to please any grown-up who came along. The grown-ups never seemed so very anxious to please the children.

"Do you see the children in the classroom?" the girl was asking. "They are all at school."

"School," said Joe, nodding.

"They've got some pets," said Bel. "Animals. What animal can you see?"

Joe nodded again. "See. Animals."

Bel held the book up so that Sarah could see the pictures as well.

"Can you see the animals too?" she asked.

Sarah looked at the page. She could see a hamster, a goldfish, a canary, a caterpillar in a jam-jar and a brown and white animal in a cage. It was quite a nice picture. Perhaps this girl was not so very useless. Sarah smiled up at her.

"What's this one, Joe?" Bel asked, pointing to the fish.

"Water," whispered Joe.

"That's right," said Bel, anxious not to discourage him. "It's a bowl of water, and there is something swimming in it. Do you know what it is?"

Goldfish! Sarah shouted.

Mrs Hinksey came over. "It's probably best if you just deal with Joe," she said. "One child will be enough for you to handle at the moment, and Sarah is a bit excitable. There's no point in showing her pictures. That's a bit advanced for her. I'm afraid she understands very little."

Bel smiled apologetically at Sarah, just in case she should understand, and laid the book flat on her lap. "It's a goldfish, Joe, and here is a little bird."

"Bird," said Joe. He looked at Bel's face more than at the book, and she was careful to smile and nod at him to show that he was doing well. He repeated every word that she said. They turned over to a

20

picture of the playground. Bel made her fingers walk up the ladder and said "Whee!" as she slid them down. She said it quietly, in case that was not part of Mrs Hinksey's plan. Gently she took Joe's little hand and made it go round on the roundabout. Joe's eyes shone.

"You seem to be getting on well," said Mrs Hinksey, looking over Bel's shoulder a little later. "Perhaps you could try him with his colours, would you? I have some colour cards here, and you could use those pegs on the shelf. Start with just two colours – red and yellow are probably best – and see how much he knows. Sorting is probably the easiest way to begin."

Bel fetched the pegs, with Joe following close beside her. They sat down and Bel showed Joe a heap of red pegs and a heap of yellow pegs. Sarah lay and watched. She noticed when one of the pegs fell on the floor, and tried to tell Bel to pick it up.

"Sarah, you will have to be quiet," said Mrs Hinksey, "or you will be back in your buggy and out in the passage again. Let's see, what could keep you amused?" She found a baby toy and laid it next to her. It had a mirror on it, and a bell, a squeezy rubber bulb that made a noise, and some knobs to spin.

"Have a look at that, Sarah," she said. "See if you can make the bell ring. Oh, look, one of your pegs is on the floor, Joe. Here you are."

A lady brought in the trolley with cups of coffee and plastic cups of orange squash, and announced that it was break-time.

"Have some coffee, dear," said Mrs Hinksey, coming over to Bel. "We divide up the afternoon with a drink and a short break, unless we are involved in something which it would be a pity to interrupt. But we don't take them outside in the winter, because it takes so long getting them dressed up warmly. The classes take turns to have a run-about in the hall." She sat down on the bench behind Sarah and, putting

21

her hands under Sarah's arms, lugged her to a sitting position leaning against her own knees. She had Sarah's drink in a cup with a lid, and held it up to Sarah's lips.

"You have had a long session with Joe. How did you find he got on with his colour recognition?"

"Oh, fine," said Bel. "He knows all the colours. Well, all the ordinary ones, anyway."

Mrs Hinksey smiled a little and drank her coffee.

After they had finished their squash, Bel followed the children into the hall. Duncan came and held her hand and Mrs Wallace organised a game with a huge beach ball. Sarah was brought through in her buggy. Claire passed through the hall, leading a little girl by the hand. "Hello, Bel. What's your class like?"

"It's all right," said Bel. "I've been teaching a little boy his colours. The teacher didn't realise how good he was at it. It isn't at all like what I expected. You were wrong about it not being a school for wheelchair children: look, there's that girl we saw in the park. She was in my class. I hope she didn't remember me."

"But she must have learning difficulties as well," said Claire.

"The teacher says she doesn't understand any-thing," said Bel. "I'm not sure she's right, though. She looked interested in the pictures I showed her. It looks as though her eyes are taking things in. But she doesn't seem to get taught anything. The others are all doing drawing, and fitting things together, and learning to tie laces, and counting their buttons. Loads of things."

"I'd better go," said Claire. "We're supposed to be fetching something from one of the classes up the other end. Your kids are bigger than mine. These little ones have only just started. We have to sit them on their potties every half hour. But they are really sweet. They play with sand and water and things, and I'm supposed to talk to them about it to help their language development."

"Not much you can say about sand," Bel giggled. "Sandy."

Claire looked important. "Well, there is wet sand and dry sand, and it can be soft or hard or sticky, and of course they play with scoops and buckets and things, so you talk about them being full and empty, trickling, pouring, building, squashing. There is quite a wide vocabulary, actually."

"Did you drink the coffee?" Bel asked. She knew that Claire hated coffee.

Claire nodded. "I put in four sugars to drown the taste. I didn't bother saying anything, because they probably won't offer us one usually, if we're busy with trips and things. I'd rather have had a bottle of milk. I used to enjoy that at primary school, with a straw. Do you think we are supposed to pay for the coffee?"

Mrs Hinksey came out into the hall and Claire disappeared. "Hello, Isabel," she said. "I wondered if you could come and help me move the tables?" Bel followed Mrs Hinksey back to the classroom. They pushed the little tables together in the centre of the room, and arranged the chairs round them. "I suppose we had better leave space for Sarah's buggy," said Mrs Hinksey. "The other children don't like to see her left out."

"Doesn't she understand anything?" asked Bel. "She doesn't look stupid."

"I'm afraid she's what they used to call a vegetable," said Mrs Hinksey. "We try to keep her happy, and I believe she does make fewer of those awful noises than when she started here. It doesn't do these children any good to let them behave in ways that will frighten the public when they go outside. But that is about all we have achieved. Of course she might make more progress with intensive one-to-one care, but this

23

class has had rather bad luck with teachers chopping and changing. I only moved here in September myself, and it takes a while to get to know all the children. Besides, there never is time to fit in everything one wants to do. Our classes seem small, but all the children need more help than we can give them. If I'm forced to make a choice, I have to choose in favour of the children who will be able to get something out of life, in however limited a way. No-one has managed to make any headway with Sarah. I do set aside a little time each day to do something with her, but it's like a drop in the ocean. She seems to enjoy the swimming. They all go swimming at least once a week. It's easier for some of them to move in the water than on dry land, where they have to support their whole weight."

The children came in from the playground and found their seats. Mrs Hinksey steered Sylvia to a chair and pushed her gently down on to it. Sylvia bobbed up to her feet again, but Mrs Hinksey sat her down again, and then sat herself on one of the little chairs next to her, and kept a hand lightly on her shoulder. She pointed to a chair next to Sarah's buggy for Bel.

"We're going to play our marching game today," said Mrs Hinksey. "Who remembers our marching game?"

"A little boy comes marching by, marching by, marching by, marching by," began David tunelessly. He sounded as though he might never stop.

"David remembers," said Mrs Hinksey. "Now, who is going to start? Isabel, I hope you are in good voice today. We could do with some help. Duncan, you can begin. Duncan, you know how to march round the table, don't you?" She sang, and Bel shyly joined in. "A little boy comes marching by, marching by, marching by. A little boy comes marching by, what is your name?"

Then Duncan had to sing, with some help. "My name is Duncan Stuart, Stuart, Stuart. My name is Duncan Stuart, how do you do?" At first Bel felt embarrassed singing. Not all the children sang, and Joe only whispered, so Mrs Hinksey's voice and hers rang out. Each child had a turn of marching round the table.

"Shall I push Sarah round?" Bel offered.

"All right, dear," said Mrs Hinksey. Bel took the brake off the buggy and pushed Sarah round the table, singing louder than before because she was singing for her. When they reached the part about her name, Sarah began to kick her legs and shout. Bel was afraid that Mrs Hinksey would tell her off, but she seemed to think that it was all right for her to make a noise when they were all singing. It really did sound a little like 'Sarah Anscombe', which was her name.

When Willowbank's day ended, Bel and Claire had to go back to their own school which ended half an hour later. As the children got their coats on, Mrs Hinksey called Bel over to the quiet corner. Joe was standing by her.

"I was going to say nothing," she said. "But I thought I had better just give you a little warning against expecting too much of these children. Now, Joe, here are some coloured pegs. Can you show me a red one?"

Joe looked anxiously into Mrs Hinksey's face, and took up a green peg.

"Thank you, Joe," she said. "Now a yellow one, please."

Joe picked up a red peg.

"And what colour is this one?" Mrs Hinksey asked, showing him a yellow peg.

"Peg," whispered Joe. "Colour."

"Well done, Joe," she said heartily, patting him on the shoulder. "Run along and fetch your coat."

"I don't understand," said Bel. "I was sure he could to it."

"I'm quite sure you did think he could do it," said Mrs Hinksey. "It's easy to make mistakes if you really want to believe the children have some ability or other. "I'm pleased that you are interested enough in my children to want them to achieve. But it's slower work than that, I'm afraid."

"He definitely could match the colours," said Bel. "We started with that."

"Yes, he probably could," said Mrs Hinksey. "And maybe one day," she added kindly, "you will teach him to recognise them all by name. But in this job we have to be very objective and very analytical and take things one step at a time. Anyway, it's time you were getting back to school, now. Thank you for your help, and we'll look forward to seeing you next Wednesday."

Bel felt that she would never want to come here again. She wanted to go and hide somewhere for a hundred years. How could she have told Mrs Hinksey that she had taught Joe his colours, and it turned out that he did not know them at all? Had she really made it up? She tried to think back to their session with the coloured pegs. What had Joe said or done that had made her think that he knew the colours? She felt that she had cheated Joe, by somehow using him to make herself feel good, to convince herself that she could be a great teacher.

Sarah, waiting in the hall to be wheeled home, saw Bel hurry through the main entrance. Her face was even pinker now, almost red. She looked as though she might cry, except that she was grown up, and grown-ups don't cry.

Claire was waiting for Bel outside. "Come on," she called. "We'll be late back. I wish they'd let us go straight home."

Bel looked at Claire, and remembered that she had told her that she had taught Joe his colours.

"How did you like it?" asked Claire. 'You don't wish we had done the playgroup now, do you?"

They set off down the drive.

"That little boy that I told you about," Bel said quickly. "He didn't know his colours after all. I just thought he did. It was so embarrassing."

Claire looked blankly at her, then shrugged her shoulders. "I wonder why it's so important for them to be taught the names of colours? The main thing is that they can see them, isn't it?"

"Did you get on all right?" Bel asked.

"Oh, it was really good," said Claire. "The little ones are so sweet, Bel, you would love them. We played singing games with them, and I looked after a little boy called Kim. I can't see that there's anything wrong with him, really. I mean, he could clap his hands in the right places, and touch his toes when the song said so. He seemed really bright to me."

"How old is he?" Bel asked, glad to forget the last conversation with Mrs Hinksey.

"Three, nearly four," said Claire. "They take them at nursery age, you see, to give them an extra start."

Bel thought about her neighbours' three-year-old, who could swing upside down on the gate and tell rude jokes. Touching toes and clapping hands would not make Claire's little Kim normal. Claire was doing the same thing that she had done, willing the children to be all right and not noticing what was wrong with them. Bel told herself that from now on she would be objective and analytical.

"We've got to write it up this evening," Claire reminded her. "I've got loads to write. I'm going to do it like a story, and this will be the first chapter, my first visit. How are you going to do it?"

Bel thought for a moment. "A loose-leaf folder," she

decided. "With a page for each child. And I shall write down anything that I have been told about the child on one side of the page, and things that I have observed on the other side."

"Nothing about how you feel about them?" asked Claire.

"Not until I've finished, at the end of the term," said Bel. "Then maybe one little section about that. First I'm going to find out about them.

5 At Bel's

Bel spent most of her Saturdays at Claire's father's house, or out on one of the trips that he organised, and Bel's Mum felt she should have Claire round in return. She felt guilty if Claire didn't come round for tea at least once during the week.

When they got home to Bel's flat the following Wednesday, Mum was arranging slices of mushroom on top of a pizza.

"That looks nice, doesn't it?" she said, standing back to look at the pattern she had made.

"It does," said Bel. "It's a pity Claire doesn't like mushrooms."

Mum looked up at Claire in horror. "I thought it was red peppers? I specially didn't put red peppers on."

"Yes," said Claire. "I don't like red peppers."

"But you don't like mushrooms either?" said Mum.

"It's all right," said Bel. "I can eat hers."

Mum slid the pizza into the oven and washed her hands. "And I suppose Gilly will say she doesn't want any," she said. "You eat salad, anyway, don't you, Claire? So how was your community thing today? Better than last week, Bel?"

Claire looked at Bel in surprise. "What was wrong with last week? I thought it was all right?"

"I told you," said Bel. "I thought I'd taught that little Joe his colours, and the teacher told me I was stupid and I'd got it all wrong."

"Oh, yes," said Claire vaguely. "I didn't know you were so upset about it."

"I wasn't so very upset," said Bel. "Anyway, I am going to teach him. Whenever I spoke to him today I mentioned the colour of something. I said, 'That's a nice green jumper you're wearing', and 'Drink up your white milk'."

"You must have sounded crazy," said Claire. She caught Bel's eye, and added, "But it's a good idea. I expect he'll pick them up ever so quickly if you keep on doing that."

"Pass me that brown spoon, Bel," said Mum. "Not that one, dumbo, it's silver. Well, greyish silver. The brown wooden one. We have to teach you your colours. How about you, Claire? Did you have a good afternoon there?"

"It was great," said Claire. "My group are doing work on where food comes from, and we took them out to a farm to see the cows and tractors and things, all in their wellies. They were terribly excited. The farmer was really nice. She let them all have a go sitting on the tractor, and then she actually drove them around a bit in a cart behind the tractor. The boy I was supposed to be looking after kept trying to stand up, and I thought he was going to jump out. And there were some lambs. Some of the children fed them from bottles. I wouldn't have minded having a go. I've never done that. And just before we left she gave them all a drink of milk. She pretended it was fresh from the cows, but it wasn't really, because the teacher didn't think they should have it unpasteurised."

"Did you mind being with the big ones?" Bel asked. "I'd feel a bit strange being in charge of people older than me."

"I was really shocked at first," said Claire. "I was expecting to be with the little ones again. But they

30

were nice, and several of them are smaller than average for their age anyway. They're a funny mixture, because some of them are just like younger children, big babies, and some of them really are like people of our age, proper teenagers, just sort of simpler. One girl kept talking to me about where I buy my clothes and where I get my hair cut and all that. She didn't speak very clearly, but it was almost the sort of conversation that people have at school."

"I was mostly with the same children as last week," said Bel. "It's nice. I'm getting to know them."

"Is it all trips?" Mum asked. "Where did you take your lot?"

"We didn't go anywhere, but we had a seaside day. It was really good."

"Seaside? At this time of year?"

"Well, we borrowed an extra sandpit and had a wet one and a dry one, and we built castles and things. That was my job. And they made sandwiches and had a picnic all sitting on the floor. And some posh woman who helps sometimes brought a pony and a donkey to the school, and they all had rides round the playground. I think your big ones saw them in the morning, Claire, to go with their farm business. That was the big treat. Oh, yes, we had loads of shells to look at as well, and we listened to a tape of seaside noises, boats and seagulls and stuff."

"Did they enjoy it?" asked Claire. "Did they understand about the seaside?"

"I'm not sure," said Bel. "Most of them can't talk enough for you to know exactly what they're thinking. Mrs Hinksey had photographs of some of them when they went on a trip to the seaside last summer, but you can't tell whether they know what the photographs are. I'd have thought it would be more sensible to do a seaside day in the summer, maybe just after a trip, or just before one so that they know what to expect. But Mrs Hinksey said it made a nice break in the middle of winter."

"So you played in the sandpit all afternoon?"

"I wasn't just playing! I had to stop Sylvia scooping it all out on to the floor, and try to persuade David to lift the bucket up after he'd been patting the sand out for half an hour, and help Duncan make a proper castle with shells round it, and protect it from being bashed down by the others, and all the time I was supposed to be talking to them with educational words, like you were on about last week, *damp* and *trickling* and *pouring* and all that. And of course I was talking about red buckets and yellow spades to Joe. And I persuaded Mrs Hinksey to let Sarah have a go at the sand too."

The front door slammed.

"Hello, Gilly!" Mum called.

Bel waited for the door of their bedroom to slam. Usually Gilly shut herself in straight away without even returning Mum's greeting. Bel had given up saying hello to her.

"Hi, Mum!" Gilly called from the hall.

Mum raised her eyebrows, then smiled. Gilly came into the kitchen. "Hi, Claire. Hi, Bel. All right if Godfrey's here for tea, Mum?" she added casually.

"Yes, of course," said Mum. "Hello, Godfrey. Nice to see you again." Bel saw her looking anxiously at the oven, mentally dividing the pizza into five pieces.

"Smells good," said Godfrey. "Anything I can do to help?"

"All under control, thanks, Godfrey," said Mum. "Oh, you could get the celery out of the fridge and chop a bit up to put in the salad."

"What about an apple as well?" Bel suggested, trying to help make the tea large enough for five. "Here, I'll do it."

"So what was that about Sarah?" Claire asked.

"Why didn't Mrs Hinksey want her to have a go in the sand?"

"Oh, is this your community project?" said Gilly. "How are you getting on with it?" Sometimes when she was feeling friendly she sounded like an aunt. "Do you remember our project, Godfrey? Making that raised garden at the old people's home? That old man kept coming out to talk to us, and then Miss Radcot told us off for stopping work."

"You made the cement all sloppy," said Godfrey. "Useless." He gave Gilly a nudge, which was the most he dared touch her in front of Mum. "This all right?" He tipped the chopped celery into the salad bowl.

"Come on," said Gilly. "We'd better get a bit of work done before tea." She led him off to the bedroom. "All right if Godfrey uses your desk, Bel?" she called over her shoulder.

"All right," said Bel.

"Go on," said Claire.

"What?"

"Sarah and the sand."

"Oh yes. Well, you know what Sarah's like, all folded up in her buggy. She can't reach the sand-trays because they're level with her head, and anyway Mrs Hinksey says she doesn't understand anything. But I thought that if she's just a baby inside, she should be allowed to play with the sort of things that babies like, and babies love sand, don't they, Mum?"

"Well, once they get big enough not to get it in their mouths," said Mum, remembering seaside holidays with Gilly and Bel.

"Well, Sarah can't put anything in her mouth even if she wants to," said Bel. "So I said couldn't I put some sand in a tray on the floor for her to play with, and Mrs Hinksey said it was silver sand, and expensive, and she didn't want it wasted, and she was a bit huffy about Sarah being lucky to have someone to take such an interest in her. She doesn't like me talking to Sarah. But it's horrible for her to be left out all the time."

"Well, I suppose if she is just like a baby, it's a bit of a waste of time," said Mum.

"Go on, Mum!" said Bel indignantly. "I've seen you with babies! You talk to them all the time, and show them things, and get them to try out things, even if they don't give any sign of understanding. You told Mary that she had to do a Christmas stocking for Kieran, and he wasn't even a month old!"

"Well, anyway, did she let you do it?"

"Yes, we put Sarah down on the mat, and I got a tray of the dry sand and put it next to her, and she just lay and looked at it as though she was waiting for something to happen. I had to get her to enjoy it, just to show Mrs Hinksey, so I got some plastic cups and spoons and things. I couldn't nick the proper sand stuff from the other children. She was looking sort of sulky. I think she was fed up with hearing that sand was what babies liked. She didn't like being called a baby."

"Come on, Bel," said Claire. "She's not capable of being upset about things like that. She's probably got an I.Q. of about zero."

"Wait a bit," said Bel. "I talked to her about where the sand came from. I felt a bit of an idiot, but I thought that was better than risking insulting her by treating her as an idiot. I trickled sand over her hand, and she just looked really blank. Usually she smiles if you pay her any attention, so I'm sure she was cross about being called a baby."

"So she didn't do anything," said Claire, "and you think that proves that she's intelligent."

"Shut up a minute," said Bel. "I got some water to make it gungey, and just as I was about to pour it in, I thought I ought to give her the choice, so I asked her, 'Do you want water in it?' and she pulled her head right back. And then she did that again when I asked if she wanted to pour it in herself."

"That's why you keep pulling your head back, is it?" said Claire. "I was feeling sorry for you. I thought you had a stiff neck."

"But how could she pour the water herself?" Mum asked, getting knives and forks from the drawer. "I thought she couldn't do anything."

"Well, I helped her lift up her arm so that she could tip the jug over, and the water poured out into the sand. And then I propped her up against me so that she could see into the tray, and she started banging it and nearly tipped it up. I only just caught it in time."

"Sounds like a baby to me," said Claire.

"I made sand-pies for her to knock down. All right, so that's what babies do, but she was knocking them down, sometimes with a great big swipe of her arm, and according to Mrs Hinksey she can't do anything at all. And she was loving it. Mrs Hinksey came over and admitted that she'd been wrong. She said 'I'm pleased that you have found something that Sarah can enjoy at her own level'. But then when it came to clearing up I started to think that her level isn't so low after all. I got another jug of water and poured it over her right hand, which was the sandy one, and she just flipped it back into the tray so that it got all sandy again. And when I frowned at her, she really grinned. She was doing it on purpose. And I said, 'Are you trying to make me late getting back to my school?', because it was the end of the day by then and we were supposed to be clearing up, and she pulled her head right back again, for 'Yes', you see. So I think she could talk, in a way, if I could work out a way to do it."

"What are you on about?" said Claire. "Either she can talk or she can't. You can't do it for her."

"Oh, I know she can't actually speak," said Bel. "But there are several things that she can do. She can pull her head back, and she can make her hand go more or less where she wants it to. Maybe she could point to words if I wrote them down, so that I would know what she was trying to say."

Claire laughed. "She's a genius, then, is she? You know that hardly any of the kids in that school can read, never mind the ones that can't even talk?"

"Well, I would have to teach her to read first, then," Bel persisted. "Or maybe pictures. She could point to a picture of a cup if she wanted a drink, or a picture of a buggy if she wanted to get in her buggy."

"But it's up to the teacher whether she does those things, isn't it?" said Mum. "She can't really choose, and nor can you. Anyway, I don't see how you would do it. Did you talk to the teacher about it?"

"No," said Bel. "It's no good. She's quite nice to Sarah, but she is sure that she is just a baby inside, and if Sarah did find a way of saying things, it would hurt Mrs Hinksey's feelings, because she is the teacher and she should know what all the children are able to do."

"Well, she probably does," said Claire. "You can see she's been at the job for years."

"I should think this pizza is just about ready," said Mum. "Call Gilly and Godfrey, will you, Bel?"

Bel left the kitchen, reminding herself that the way her ideas were being ignored now was only a hundredth, a thousandth as bad as the way Sarah's ideas and thoughts and wishes were being ignored every minute of every day. If she had ideas or thoughts or wishes.

6 Snowdrop House

Sarah lay awake in her cot. She could not understand why the other children had fallen asleep. There were four others in her room, and they were all sleeping soundly. Sarah was never tired when they put her to bed, because sitting in a buggy or lying on the floor only makes you weary, not properly tired, and she was used to looking at half of the room and listening to the quiet sounds downstairs.

The older children's television programme had been switched off. Sarah knew what it was, because she had heard them talking about it at teatime. She listened for the music at the end, and heard baths being run and people complaining about having their teeth brushed. Now it was all quiet in the big ones' room. They were probably asleep as well. By now the night staff would have come on duty. Sarah hoped it was not Mrs Churchill's turn.

Sarah thought back over the day. The donkey and the horse were nice. She wished she could have had a ride. She imagined herself galloping round the playground, not being led slowly like the others. She wondered why Mrs Hinksey had made them all sit on the floor to eat the sandwiches. Something to do with the seaside. The sand had been fun. That Isabel was quite nice. She'd said sensible things about the sand, although nothing new.

"You can dig in it with the spoon if you want," she had said. "But it's not really for eating. It's like very

37

tiny bits of rock, that the sea has smashed into little grains. It feels horrible if you get it in your mouth."

Sarah could have told her that. She had seen the fuss that David made, a few days before, when he had absent-mindedly put a handful of sand in his mouth. Mrs Hinksey had tried to clean it out with a tissue, but David had kept on spitting for an hour afterwards, trying to get out the last grains.

One of the babies woke up and cried and Sarah heard someone hushing it. People were talking quietly outside. It was probably Davina and Mrs Eaton chatting before Davina went home. Mrs Eaton lived in the flat upstairs, so she hadn't far to go home. Sarah knew that Davina lived two bus journeys away. Sarah had never been on a bus herself, of course, but Davina had pointed them out to her.

Sarah heard Davina call, "Goodnight" to Mrs Eaton, and then she must have thought of something else to say, because she heard her voice again, close to the house.

Sarah was too hot. The radiators were always on. She did not want pyjamas on, and she did not want the blanket over her. Duncan had pushed his blanket off and was lying back looking so comfortable with his arms stretched across the bed. Sylvia slept like a mouse. They gave her medicine to make her sleep soundly and it was only towards the morning that she began to toss about. Davina had put Sarah on her right side so she could not see Joe. One of the night staff would come in soon to turn her over.

First whoever it was made a cup of tea. They only ran the tap for a minute but Sarah heard the water roaring in the pipe, and the kettle whistling for an instant before it was snatched off the ring. Then the television was switched on, and changed from channel to channel. Then Sarah heard the steps on the stairs. She heard them go into the big ones' room, which was nearer the stairs. All quiet in there. Then they came into Sarah's room. Mrs Churchill. Sarah whimpered.

"Hello, Sarie," she whispered. "Not asleep, then?"

She turned Sarah over. She was gentle with her hands. It was strange that she should be. She made Sarah's pillow comfortable. It was a thin pillow, so that she shouldn't suffocate in it, but Mrs Churchill plumped it up as well as she could. She wound up the musical box on the cot. Sarah wanted so much to like her. She was kind in a way. Sarah wished that the other thing she knew about her was not true. She wished that she would just check the other children and go straight on to the babies' room. For a minute it seemed that she was going to, but then she turned back to Sarah.

"You can't tell on me, can you, Sarie?" she whispered in her kind voice. Sarah hated it when she said that, because it made her feel that it was her fault for keeping the secret, as though she was saying nothing on purpose.

Mrs Churchill went to Joe's locker and opened it. Joe had a plastic teddy-bear money-box. Very quietly, without letting the coins jangle a bit, she took off the bear's head and took out a coin. Then she screwed the head back on and put the bear back in the locker. The coin went into her trouser pocket.

Timothy's money box always had the most money in it. He was older than the others in the room and he knew how much money was in his box. Sarah hated it when Timothy discovered that money was missing. It would be on Saturday, when they were taken down to the shops. No-one would believe Timothy when he said that money had gone missing. It was a joke at Snowdrop House that he always thought his money had been stolen. "Anyone been at your money-box this week, Timothy?" they would tease him. No-one knew how much he had because the gardener would give him money sometimes for helping him, and his nan gave him extra pocket money when she came to visit. Mrs Eaton had offered to keep the box for him in her office, but Timothy would not let it out of his locker. He thought it was safe there.

Duncan had a five-pound note this week that his uncle had sent for his birthday. Mrs Churchill decided that it would be noticed if that went missing, and only took a few coins. Sylvia did not have a money box. Mrs Eaton looked after all her pocket money, and chose how to spend it for her. It was the same for Sarah, so Mrs Churchill could not steal anything from either of them. Mrs Eaton had bought the musical box with Sarah's money. It was quite nice at first, but now she was sick of the jangling tune. Mostly Mrs Eaton bought her clothes, and sometimes posters to stick on the wall by her cot. She liked the one of the baby fox. It was called a cub. Davina had told her.

Mrs Churchill patted Sarah and tiptoed down the hall to the babies' room. Then Sarah heard her go downstairs. The first time that she had seen her take the children's money, she shouted for help. Police! Thief! Help! Help! Help! Mrs Eaton heard from the flat upstairs and came running down to see what was the matter. Mrs Churchill was flustered. The money was already in her pocket. Together, the women poured two spoonfuls of yellow medicine down Sarah's throat. It made her dizzy, and then she floated away to sleep. The next time she did not bother to shout. The words came out wrong in any case, although Duncan might have understood if he had been awake.

40

7 At Claire's

On Saturday it poured with rain, and it was cold as well. Claire's father, Russell, hired a video for them to watch, and made the front room into a cinema. He pulled the curtains shut against the miserable grey outside world, and brought in bowls of salty popcorn for them to eat. Russell wouldn't let them watch adult films, because of Paul being so young, but he was clever at choosing interesting films that didn't seem babyish. Today he'd got one out about a gang of teenagers trying to stop a row of houses being demolished for a new road. He came and watched it with them and laughed until he cried over the pin-striped politician who was trying to get the road built. Then he told them to stop the video for a minute and raced out of the house. He came back panting and sweating with a load of chocolate. Paul would not have any. He said it was stupid to eat things that you knew were bad for you.

Bel almost felt sad when she had a good time with Russell. It was so different from her own flat when her father was at home. He had the television on all the time, on whatever programme he chose, which was always boring, and he would send Gilly or, more often, Bel running to the shops to get a paper or a packet of cigarettes. Bel could not imagine him running out to get a treat for them. It was good that he worked in Scotland and did not spend much time at home.

Russell always sat with Paul to watch television. If Paul was in the armchair, Russell would perch on the arm and put his hand on Paul's shoulder. If Paul was on the floor, Russell would flop down next to him. Bel felt sorry for Russell. He was trying to make up for the lost week, trying to stay close to Paul in spite of seeing him only on Saturdays, but Paul was not the sort of child to respond to that. He was glad to have his father there, but only to bounce his own ideas off. "That couldn't really happen, Dad, could it?" Or, "I know how they filmed that bit. I bet she wasn't really leaning out of the top floor window."

"Shut up, Paul," Claire said quite often. "We're trying to watch it."

Then Russell would whisper his answer to Paul's comment. Bel watched them almost as much as she watched the film. It was strange to see a parent trying so hard to be a parent. Bel's own mum never seemed to think about being a mother. She put up with Gilly's moodiness as long as she could, trying to be understanding, then at last she would snap. After the row, she might apologise in words or with some sort of treat, and things would be back to normal again. She sometimes used the fact of being a mother as an excuse for bullying Gilly or Bel about putting on warm clothes, or doing their homework properly, but she did not need to watch films with them in order to feel like their mother.

The thought went through Bel's mind that not all fathers could be as persistent as Paul's. Some fathers might give up, and accept that the child they did not often see had become almost a stranger. She wondered for a second whether, when she and Gilly were little, her own father had perhaps tried to be close to them, and then given up because their life with Mum was so settled and self-sufficient. It was really as though they did not need him. She might have spent time wondering whether she should feel sorry for him, if just then the demolition team had not appeared on the screen, ready to knock down the first of the houses. A brave girl stood in the doorway, her hands on her hips, defying the workmen.

"They'll just go and move her," said Paul. "She's not really brave. She knows they can't really knock the house down on top of her."

8   Willowbank School

On Wednesday afternoon Bel was reminded about
parents trying to keep in touch with their children. It
was her children's turn in the multi-sensory room,
which sounded exciting until Mrs Hinksey told her
that her job would be to help the children take
off their shoes, jumpers and any jewellery and look
after them until it was their turn to go in – experts
were hidden away in the mysterious room ready
to help the children to listen or make sounds, to
bounce and develop their coordination, or to notice
and react to wonderful lights flashing off the ceiling
and walls.

"It's very helpful to have you here," said Mrs Hinksey. "Normally I have to stay in the classroom with
the children, but with you and Mrs Tennyson both
here, I can be in the multi-sensory room and the
children can have longer turns. I've set out some
colouring for them to do while they are waiting."

Mrs Tennyson was Sylvia's mother who had come
in to help. Somehow Bel had imagined that these
children would have parents like themselves, not
handicapped of course, but the large slow ones would
have large slow parents, and quicksilver Sylvia would
have a restless, fast-moving mother, also with close-
cropped hair and perhaps similar clothes, a simple
track-suit and pull-on shoes. But Mrs Tennyson was
a little overweight and very tired-looking. Her clothes
were rather fancy, a lacy collar and cuffs on her

blouse, and beads embroidered on her cardigan. She sat on one of the small chairs in the classroom and did not look as though she would ever be able to get up from it.

She was full of admiration for Mrs Hinksey.

"She's only had them a term, you know, but she knows them inside out already. You have to know what you're at with my Sylvia. She won't respond to everyone, but she'll listen to Mrs Hinksey. Mrs Hinksey rings us up to let us know what she's working on with Sylvia, and the progress Sylvia's made. Of course, she's very experienced. Worked for years at a similar school in Sussex before her husband had to move up here. I'm glad Sylvia's in her class."

There were only six children in the class. The others had already padded away in their socks to have fun in the multi-sensory room. Bel encouraged the children to sit down to their colouring.

Mrs Hinksey had left the door open, so that the teacher next door could come in and help in any emergency. There was a table across the doorway to prevent Sylvia from dashing out into the corridor. Sylvia could have jumped over it in a second, or squirmed underneath, but the table was enough to remind her to stay in the classroom. One moment she would be sitting in her place, colouring in the shapes in her work-book, and a moment later she would be hovering near the open door, longing to be racing in huge circles out in the hall. Her colouring followed her wishes: big loops of crayon that took no notice of the shapes they should have been filling.

"You can see why we couldn't have her at home," Mrs Tennyson said apologetically to Bel, who had just retrieved her. "It's a full-time job keepng an eye on her, and I've three younger ones at home. That's why I try and come in during school-time, when my little one's at playgroup, so that I can keep in touch. You like your mummy to come in and see you, don't you, Sylvia?"

For a moment Sylvia looked her in the eye and a smile flashed across her face, and then she was focussed on something else, far away, and struggled to her feet.

"No, darling, sit down and do your nice colouring."

"Doesn't she live at home, then?" Bel asked cautiously.

"No, she's at Snowdrop House. It's ever such a nice place, they take really good care of them. There are several of them there. Joe lives at Snowdrop House, don't you, Joe?" Joe chewed his crayon and looked up anxiously. "And Duncan over there, poor little fellow. His mother died, you know, and all the children are in care. He's one of the few that don't ever get to go home at weekends or Christmas. Of course we have Sylvia home at Christmas, and for some of the holidays. I'd hate her to think we'd abandoned her."

Duncan could colour quite nicely, but he preferred to talk. "You want a different colour now, Joe? What about yellow? Oh, you need a tissue. I'll go and get you one."

"Now you sit down, Duncan, there's a love," said Mrs Tennyson. "Joe can fetch it for himself. That's right, Joe. Good boy." For all Mrs Tennyson looked so floppy, Bel realised that she could learn from her.

David coloured hard. His knuckles went white, the crayon was gripped so tightly. If Bel did not tell him when to move on, he would colour over the same part of the shape so often that the crayon would go right through the paper. Sarah liked David's bright hard patches, but she wanted them to go right up to the edges of the lines, and fill in the shapes properly. She watched Joe's faint lines gently criss-cross the shape on the paper. Joe was too slow. It was frustrating to watch him.

46

Bel sat by Sylvia until she had finished her colouring. Then she was allowed to play in the sand. When David's crayon had gone through the paper three times he was allowed to stop too. Joe carried on colouring lightly while he peered up into Bel's face to see if he was doing it right, and while he looked away the faint lines went all over the paper. Duncan scolded him for it, and was the last to finish.

"Oh, and there's another one," said Mrs Tennyson. "I forgot about Sarah. She's been at Snowdrop House since Sylvia started there. Poor little girl. Seeing her makes me realise that we're not the only ones with problems. At least Sylvia can get about."

Bel fetched Sylvia from the cupboard, returned her to the table, and went to put back the puzzles that she had dragged to the floor.

"I can do the puzzle," said David, jumping up. "I can do the puzzle."

Bel looked hopelessly at the bright pieces mixed in a heap. She decided that as they were basically minding the children, it did not matter much whether David was doing colouring or jigsaw puzzles, but she was not sure that he could manage it. She helped him pick up the pieces and sat him at a table to try to put them back into their frames.

Sarah was in her buggy, pushed close up against the table. Bel tried to help her colour some shapes. She held the paper down flat with one hand (Sarah did not have a work book of her own), and tried to guide Sarah's hand and the crayon with the other. It was hopeless. Sarah's arm bent the wrong way and the crayon flew across the table.

"It's no good, dear," said Mrs Tennyson. "Just let her watch. She can see the bright colours."

Bel thought that a blackboard would be easier, because it would not crumple up the way the paper did. She fetched Sylvia back from the door, and reminded Duncan that he was supposed to be colouring.

"Shall I colour a shape in for you, Sarah?" she asked.

Sarah gave a huge smile, so Bel pulled the sheet of paper towards her. She picked a crayon from the margarine tub in the centre of the table, then she put it back again. "I don't know which colour you want, Sarah," she said. She showed her one crayon after another, but her smile was so wide that Bel could not tell if she preferred one colour to another. It made a change for Sarah to be asked what she wanted, although people often pretended to ask her questions. "Shall we get you up now, Sarah?" "Do you want your nice egg now, Sarah?" "You can't wait to get to school, can you, Sarah?"

"You'll have to do something to show me the one you want," said Bel. "What can you do to say yes?"

Sarah pulled her head back as far as it would go. Bel felt triumphant. She had known the gesture meant yes. She looked round to see whether Mrs Tennyson was watching, but Mrs Tennyson was holding Sylvia on her lap, trapped by her warm knitted arms, and at the same time talking to Duncan about his picture.

"All right," said Bel. "Do you want me to use this blue crayon?"

Sarah kept very still.

Mrs Hinksey came back from the multi-sensory room with the three children who had finished their turn. "We're ready for Duncan now, and David. Caroline from Mr Barton's class is coming in too. Oh, you are doing a puzzle are you, David. Three puzzles? I think really one at a time would be more sensible."

The comment was said to David, but aimed at Bel. Bel did not feel she could explain. "Do you want the yellow one?" she asked Sarah quietly.

"I think it would be most helpful if you concentrated on the other children, Bel," said Mrs Hinksey. "Sarah does love attention, but Joe needs quite a lot of help with his colouring, and look, Sylvia is over by the window."

Mrs Tennyson had slid Sylvia off her lap as Mrs Hinksey came in, afraid of being seen to favour her, or ignore the others.

"Oh, I'm sorry," said Bel. She fetched Sylvia gently back to her place, told Joe that he was doing well, and helped David to put the last few pieces into the puzzle trays. David and Duncan went off excitedly with Mrs Hinksey, and Bel and Mrs Tennyson helped the other children to put their shoes back on. Bel was buckling a little girl's sandals for her when she saw that Mrs Tennyson was making the boy do his own laces.

"That's it, push the end through there. Now you can pull it tight. Aren't you a clever boy!"

Bel got the little girl to push the ends of the straps through the buckles, and do some of her buttons herself. She found her workbook, got her started with a blue crayon, and then she thought that she could go back to Sarah. But Sarah was ignoring her now and did not even smile when Bel showed her the other crayons. Perhaps she was cross with her for stopping in the middle of the conversation. Or perhaps Mrs Hinksey was right to treat her as someone with the mind of a baby, who just liked to see bright colours. She could have been smiling earlier at anything, and the movement of her head might have meant nothing.

9   Willowbank School

Miss Radcot, the social studies teacher at Bel's school, had a packed schedule on Wednesday afternoons. First she had to drive two boys out to the geriatric hospital, and then she visited one or two of the other groups of children at their community placements. She had been several times to supervise the building of a tree-house at the playgroup, because you could not risk them making a shoddy job of it. Of course, the playgroup parents were meant to be helping, but Miss Radcot was afraid that the school could be sued if the house collapsed when the toddlers were climbing in it. The boys at the old people's home needed watching, and Jeehan and Rebecca had been reported for being rude to customers at the Hospice Shop. So it was the last Wednesday before half term before she got round to visiting the girls at the special school, who were quiet and sensible and were probably well supervised by the school staff.

Claire was in the little ones' classroom. They were waiting to go swimming, and Claire was helping them all to check that they had their swimming costumes and towels in their bags. Soon after Miss Radcot arrived, Claire very efficiently bustled one of the children off to the toilet. On her way back, she stopped to tickle a small boy who was lying on a bean bag, and give him back a toy that he had dropped. Miss Radcot was impressed. She talked to the class teacher, who was grateful for Claire's help. She talked to

Claire, and heard that she was thinking of making a career of special education when she left school. Miss Radcot glowed, thinking how very valuable these community projects often turned out to be. Then she moved on to Mrs Hinksey's class.

Miss Radcot remembered from last term, when another set of children had done their community project at this school, that Mrs Hinksey was a very organised teacher whose class was always quiet and orderly. Today they were sitting at their tables with a blob of dough each. Mrs Hinksey was talking about 'fat' and 'thin' and they were making fat and thin shapes. David's thin shapes were like pieces of string, he rolled them out so thoroughly under the palms of his hands. Joe did not press hard enough to flatten out his blob, and it stayed fat, but he whispered hopefully, "Thin? Thin?" Sylvia poked her piece wildly with her finger-tips and made it look like a sponge.

"Good morning," said Mrs Hinksey politely. These school volunteers were sometimes more trouble than they were worth, especially when their teachers started visiting as well. "We are making bread today, but as the dough has to be thoroughly kneaded, we are talking about the different shapes we can make. Well done, Duncan, that's lovely and thin."

Miss Radcot sat down on one of the small chairs and looked around. Sarah drooped in her buggy. She looked very handicapped, poor child. Isabel was nowhere to be seen.

"Isabel has some talent for teaching," said Mrs Hinksey, "as I expect you know. She has devised some ingenious aids for the children. But she has her own ideas about priorities."

Miss Radcot wondered what that meant. It was obviously a criticism. She hoped that Isabel had not been awkward. Here she came now, following a little girl into the classroom.

51

"Well, Miranda?" Mrs Hinksey said. "Have you asked Cook to turn the oven on for us?" The little girl nodded. "Well done. Come and sit down. Here is some dough for you. We have to knead it in our hands like this. Can you squeeze your dough?"

Bel sat down next to Sarah and pulled her blob of dough into two pieces. She left one a round ball, and squeezed the other one into a thin snake.

"Which one is fat, Sarah?" she asked. Sarah leant over, swung her arm across the table and landed near the round piece. Bel held her breath. "Which one is thin?"

Sarah banged the dough snake.

"Mrs Hinksey, could I show you, please?" said Bel. "She really does seem to be understanding about this."

Mrs Hinksey and Miss Radcot turned to look. The children stopped their pulling and poking and squeezing and watched Sarah.

"Which one is thin, Sarah?" Bel asked again. Sarah's shoulder was tired. She swung her arm and landed on the table, nearer the thin piece than the fat one. "Which one is fat, Sarah?"

This time she managed to land exactly on the round piece, but it was a huge effort. Sarah looked up at Mrs Hinksey. She wondered if this was to make all the difference to how people would behave towards her. Mrs Hinksey smiled. She was smiling at Bel, not at Sarah.

"I think we would require a little more proof, Isabel," she said patiently. "The first attempt was not very clear, was it? But I am pleased that Sarah is trying to point. That is quite an achievement, and we needn't worry her with concepts like thick and thin. She is trying to please you, and for Sarah that is quite a step forward."

"But that is four times she has pointed to the right one," said Bel. "And not one mistake!"

"Perhaps we could try it once more?" Miss Radcot suggested.

"Very well," said Mrs Hinksey. "I will do it myself. Now, Sarah point to the fat piece of dough."

Sarah was aching all over. The only bad thing about Wednesdays, when Isabel came and spent time with her, was that she had to sit in her buggy for so long, because Isabel brought her to join in with all the activities. Four times she had managed to answer the silly question, and here was Mrs Hinksey asking it all over again. It was no good, nobody would ever believe that she knew about things.

"Well there you are, I'm afraid, Isabel," said Mrs Hinksey, as she bent to pick up the dough that Sarah had sent flying on to the floor. "When I phrased the question slightly differently, she was completely lost, and reverted to her old behaviour. No, I'm sorry, dear, but as we discussed over the colours incident, it is only too easy to have high expectations of children, especially non-verbal children." She turned to Miss Radcot. "I'm delighted that Isabel should take such an interest in any of our pupils, but I am afraid that she isn't able to be very objective about Sarah."

Bel looked at Sarah. Her eyes were slightly crossed but she looked back at her. Bel could not tell what she was thinking. Perhaps she was not thinking anything.

Miss Radcot drove Claire and Bel back to school. She felt awkward with them. "How do you feel your community placements are going?" she asked them.

"Oh, I love it," said Claire.

"You seem to be doing very well," said Miss Radcot. "How about you, Isabel?"

Bel did not know what to say. Miss Radcot had seen her told off by Mrs Hinksey for expecting too much of Sarah.

"It's very nice that you have got so fond of the little girl in the wheelchair," Miss Radcot went on.

Bel wondered. It was true that she was fond of Sarah, but it was not her feelings about her that mattered. Sarah's whole life was so unfair. Bel hoped that even if Sarah had been some ugly kind of person that she found quite unlikeable she would still have cared enough to try to find out what she could manage to do.

"But I think Mrs Hinksey is a little worried about the extra attention that you are paying her," Miss Radcot went on as she pulled into the school car park. "She feels that it unsettles her. And of course you only have until the end of term, and then if she is capable of noticing you at all, she may feel let down when you stop visiting. Besides, in the class situation, it does make for problems if one child is singled out for attention."

"But normally she is singled out for no attention at all," said Bel. Whatever she said would be wrong, but she had to try to defend herself. "She isn't stupid, but nobody tries to find out what she can do and what she can't."

"Obviously her teacher must be the best judge of that," said Miss Radcot. "The purpose of these Wednesday afternoons is for you both to learn more about the community in which we live, and to offer practical help to others in the community, not to try to be an amateur psychologist and discover talents that the experts have failed to detect. After half term, I would like you to try to attend more to the other children, and to leave decisions about Sarah's involvement to Mrs Hinksey. This is also her request, which she asked me to pass on to you."

It was humiliating to be given a message like that by Miss Radcot. Why couldn't Mrs Hinksey have told Bel herself, and left Miss Radcot out of it? It made it look as though Bel had been really uncooperative and that Mrs Hinksey had had to call in Miss Radcot to control her. Bel felt that she would dread Wednesday afternoons from now on. What Mrs Hinksey wanted was not for Bel to treat Sarah equally, but for her to ignore Sarah.

Bel always took a lot of trouble over the other children. Joe really did know some of his colours now, and she had helped Duncan to become more independent at taking messages to different classrooms. She had taught Miranda to buckle up her own shoes and she had made hundreds of drawing sheets for David to help him learn to draw a pencil line going from left to right across the page. She prepared them at home, with a picture of a dog on the left and a bone on the right, or a bird and a nest. Mrs Hinksey had said that they were very good. She hardly spent any time with Sarah, but whenever she did, Mrs Hinksey accused her of unsettling her.

They got out of Miss Radcot's car.

"Don't look so downhearted," said Miss Radcot. "Mrs Hinksey is grateful for the work you have put in. She thinks you could make a good teacher some day. Had you thought about that at all?"

"No," said Bel. "I want to be a civil engineer." She really had no idea what she wanted to do when she finished school, but she did not want to give Miss Radcot the satisfaction of feeling that she had smoothed everything over.

On the way home Bel bought three packets of crisps and ate them one after the other, which was against the rules and which she had promised Mum never to do. After that she felt better, although they did make her feel rather sick.

Before the children went home it began to rain. Davina brought their macintoshes and Sarah's rain-cape when she came to fetch them. Sarah hated the rain-cape. It had elastic round her face which scratched, and rain trickled off the hood on to her

55

face. The grown-ups were always in a hurry to get home when it rained, so they pushed the buggy too quickly and didn't notice the bumps. Duncan fell over in a puddle and cried all the way home. Sarah was crying too, but that happened too often for anyone to take any special notice.

10 At Bel's

"How is your community thing going?" Mum asked
Bel that evening. "You haven't mentioned it for a
while."

"It's complicated," said Bel. "Mrs Hinksey, that's
the teacher that I'm usually with, is quite strict, and
she makes me feel as though I'm not being properly
helpful."

"Well, you're there to help," said Mum. "Don't you
do as she tells you?"

"It's not like that," said Bel. "She doesn't tell me
exactly what to do. Most of the time she expects me
just to know what I should be doing. If we are in the
classroom, I do know most of the routine now, and I
can take the children to the toilet, or get them washed
after painting, and things like that. I know I'm useful
then. But there's a little girl who doesn't do anything,
and Mrs Hinksey thinks she's a waste of time. She
thinks she's like a baby, and she just lies her by a
mobile, or the fish-tank, and thinks she should watch
fish all day. I mean, she does get taken swimming,
and sung to and things, but it's all baby stuff. Nobody
tries to talk to her."

"Mrs Hinksey probably knows best," said Mum.
"She is the teacher. I remember you and Claire
talking about her before. I expect the child's had her
intelligence tested and they've found that she can't
manage more than that."

"No, I asked about that," said Bel. "The school

psychologist does come round sometimes to test the children. One of the children is moving up to a different school for brighter kids, not normal, but not so handicapped, because she did well on the test. But Mrs Hinksey says that Sarah can't be tested. They write 'untestable' on her card. So the psychologist doesn't know any more about her than anybody else."

"Well, the teacher will know," said Mum. "She must have seen loads of kids like her. What is she, a mongol?"

"You shouldn't say mongol," said Bel. "It's rude to Mongolians and it's rude to the children as well, because the way they look isn't what's important."

"Crikey," said Mum. "I never can remember what they call them nowadays."

"Down's syndrome," said Bel. "But anyway, she isn't. She's got cerebral palsy, brain damage, and that doesn't tell you anything really, only that she can't get bits of herself to move properly. I just think that she could do some things if we could work out a way to help her."

"But Mrs what's-her-name reckons her brain doesn't think properly either?" asked Mum.

"Yes," said Bel indignantly. "And she hasn't got the proof! She's got no right to assume that Sarah's stupid just because she can't say anything."

"But she's probably been watching this little girl. She would have noticed any signs of intelligence. What makes you so sure that she's not stupid?"

"You can see she's not," said Bel. "She smiles, and she tries to tell you things."

"Oh, come on, Bel," said Mum. "Babies smile almost from when they're born. And they tell you things in their own way. Anyway, I don't see that it's anything to do with you what this child's I.Q. is. Just do what the teacher tells you to do. You get a certificate at the

58

end of the term, you know, if you do the community project properly."

Bel sat in her room wondering how someone could communicate with a jerk of the head and a very wild gesture with one arm. While she should have been making a list of major European rivers she began to make a list of useful words. Yes and no. Hungry and thirsty. If Sarah pointed to 'hungry', then you could show her a choice of food and she could point to the sort that she wanted. But then Bel could not offer her food in school. What could they talk about? Sarah spent most of her time watching the other children. Bel must show her the children's names. Perhaps she would know them already, from the labels on their chairs and shelves.

"What is all this?" Gilly and Godfrey had arrived home and were unpacking their bags on to Gilly's bed. "Not one of Mr Benson's bright ideas, is it? He had us colouring in these triangles once, millions and millions of them. Remember, Godfrey? They were supposed to fit all together somehow, and the class-room was full of them, but it didn't work. We must have wasted weeks and weeks on it, if you added up everyone's separate hours."

"It's to do with the community project," said Bel.

"You still doing that?" asked Gilly vaguely, sitting down next to Bel and stretching her arm under the bed. She brought out two pencils and a knitted rabbit. "Look at Bel's rabbit, Godfrey. She takes it to bed with her."

"I don't. Only when I need to. The project goes on all term. In a few weeks we're taking them for a treat at some enormous swimming pool with slides and things. It sounds brilliant. All the children are going, if they can get enough parents and people to come and help."

"So what are you doing all this for?" Gilly asked.

"There's this little girl at the school," said Bel. "I keep thinking about her. She doesn't live with her family. She lives in a home, and I thought I might go and visit her there. The teacher in her class doesn't really like me paying her special attention, so I thought it would be easier to go and see her at the home."

Gilly discovered a dried-up orange under the bed and rolled it back into the darkness. "Very energetic of you. You'll get the certificate just for doing it in school hours. Do you like the little girl so much, then?"

Bel measured out another piece of paper and carefully used her compasses to draw a large circle on it. "I thought I could go just once and see if it's better away from the school. And I'm making these to see if she can talk to me with them."

Gilly looked disbelievingly at the coloured sheets of paper. "You mean she can't even talk? What good will all this do?"

"She's brain damaged. But she can understand what people say. And she can point to things. Look, I've put the same sorts of things together on one colour. Different drinks on yellow, different toys on orange, different positions on green. Where did I put the green?"

"Different positions? What are you on about?" Gilly found half a candle under the bed. "Mum will go mad if she finds out you've been lighting candles in the bedroom!"

"I haven't," said Bel. "Claire said that candle-wax was good for your toe-nails. But it's horrible when it gets stuck underneath them. Different positions like sitting up, lying down, leaning on a cushion, that sort of thing. You see, she can't move herself either. But first of all, she'd choose which colour. So if she was thirsty, she would point to yellow on here, and then I would show her the yellow sheet with the different drinks on."

"Whew, looks complicated," said Gilly. "I don't see why they all had to be in such beautiful circles and all measured out and coloured in. Can she read?" Bel had written the words in round felt pen letters next to the pictures. For the drinks she had stuck labels on to the paper, part of a tea-packet, a coke-can label, a milk-bottle lid. She was not sure how she could give Sarah a drink, but she had made a pink sheet with a choice of food, and planned to take a few different sorts of food when she went to visit, chocolate, cheese spread, a marmite sandwich. It must be the sort of food that Sarah would not choke on.

Mum called from the kitchen, "Gilly! You'd better get on with your homework if you're planning to go out tonight!"

Godfrey was already perched on the edge of Gilly's bed, with a book on his lap, another beside him wedged open under his thigh, and an atlas on the floor.

Bel went on measuring and colouring her pieces of paper. She had thought of visiting Sarah at Snowdrop House several weeks ago, but it was a frightening prospect. It seemed like defying Mrs Hinksey, doing something behind her back, and then, what would Snowdrop House be like? The school had turned out to be less strange than Bel had feared, but it was still a strain to go there each Wednesday, wondering how friendly to be with the teachers, how tolerant to be of the children's mischief, which perhaps she should be frowning at although it generally made her giggle. While it was obvious that no-one thought of her and Claire as on a level with the children, they did not quite treat them as adults either, and it was hard to behave exactly right. Bel always dreaded going to new places and meeting new people. She ruled her lines and coloured in her charts, feeling that as long

61

as she was still busy with them she need not worry about the details of using them.

She had thought vaguely that this Saturday might be the one. Perhaps she would pluck up courage to ring Snowdrop House and arrange a visit. But to her relief, Mum provided her with an excuse.

"My God, Bel, what's this?" she exclaimed as she stared round the door at the sheets of paper spread all over the floor and bed.

"She's going to teach someone to talk with it," said Gilly. "I think she's expecting an extra big certificate, with gold writing on it."

"Something to do with that little girl?" said Mum. "How's this supposed to help her? Look, Bel, I keep forgetting to mention it, but Angela rang and said that Claire and Paul aren't going to their father's this Saturday, and you know she's working Saturdays at the supermarket, so I said they could come round here. Well, of course it's only Paul that needs babysitting, but I thought you'd like to see Claire."

"All right," said Bel.

"Well, sound a bit more enthusiastic," said Mum. "I'd like to take them somewhere nice, or give them a treat of some kind. You always do such nice things with them on Saturdays. What do you think? Would they like a museum?"

"Paul would," said Bel. "Except he probably knows all the museums inside out."

"So you don't think Claire would? Well, what about if we took the kite out? Would they enjoy that, do you think? We haven't flown it for ages. We could go up to Filkins."

Bel loved the kite. It was the sort with two strings, that could loop the loop. And Filkins Park, high above the city, was the best place for kite-flying. "Claire might think it was a bit babyish," she said. "But we could suggest it."

"Well, what would she enjoy?" Mum asked.

"We could go and look round the shops in town," said Bel. "She's always complaining that she doesn't get any time for that, because of visiting her dad every Saturday."

Mum looked disappointed.

"You could take Paul to a museum while we look round the shops," Bel suggested, "and then we could meet up at the Burger Bar or somewhere."

"I don't know if we can afford that," said Mum. "Well, I suppose we can, so long as you don't expect a whole enormous meal, just a milk shake or something. Are you sure you can't think of anything that Claire would rather do?"

"I could ask her at school tomorrow," said Bel. "But I'm sure she'd think that shopping was a treat."

Gilly sighed noisily, and shuffled some sheets of paper. Mum left.

11 Bel and Claire

Paul enjoyed Saturday. He was the only person who did. They caught a bus into town. A little girl was kneeling up on the seat in front of them, staring at them. She held her mother's ticket carefully in her woollen mitten and kept asking when she could ring the bell.

"Not yet, Tasha, I've told you. When we're nearly at our stop. Now sit round properly and don't drop that ticket."

Bel remembered that bus journeys had once been an adventure for her. "I wonder if Sarah has ever been on a bus? It would be awkward with the wheel-chair, I suppose. It must be strange to see these enormous red things driving by, and not know what they are like inside."

"She doesn't even know they have insides," said Claire.

"Of course she does!" said Bel. "She knows that you use buses to get to places. I've talked to her about it, and trains, and aeroplanes and everything."

"Oh yes!" jeered Claire. "You've taught her every-thing you know!"

Bel turned away and looked out of the window.

The gargoyles on the colleges in the high street whisked past. Mum used to point out the different monsters, the lion and monkey peeing down a drain-pipe. Bel imagined pushing Sarah along, tipping her back for a good view of all the carved creatures. She could take her into Wolsey College to see the enormous goldfish, or into Queen's College to see the giant sun-dial. On second thoughts, a sun-dial might take some explaining, and there were all those steps at the front entrance of that college. But the colleges must have some disabled students. There must be a side entrance with a ramp. If there wasn't, she would complain. She opened her mouth to say something indignant about ramps, but shut it again.

"I'd like to have a look in that shop," said Claire. "*I'll Eat My Hat.*"

"Why?"

"The shop's called *I'll Eat My Hat*, but it isn't just hats. Saskia went there the day it opened, and she said it's got some good clothes, and things like hair ties and dark glasses and stuff."

"I didn't see it," said Bel.

"It's next to the stationery shop. We could look in there as well. Mum said she'd get me some of those plastic covers to put on exercise books, and some new felt pens."

"I'm desperate for new felt pens too," said Bel. "Fat ones." Hers had run out colouring the charts for Sarah. She immediately wished she had not mentioned them, but Claire did not ask why she needed them.

The bus squealed to a stop and Claire and Bel got to their feet. The little girl in front was still asking when she could ring the bell, and Paul was still in his seat, explaining something to Mum. Mum was too polite to interrupt him. She hovered, half standing and half sitting.

"Come on, Paul," said Claire. "You'll get left on the bus."

Paul looked round at her crossly, then slid out of the seat and walked sideways down to the door, still talking. Mum nodded with a vague smile on her face.

Once they were on the pavement Mum grew brisker. "We're going to the Science Museum. Paul says it's very good, and I've never seen it."

"The Science Museum is in London, Mum," said Bel.

"It's a museum of the *history* of science," Paul said. "Old scientific instruments."

Bel saw that Paul had taken over completely. He was taking Mum to a museum, instead of the other way round.

"How long do you two want for your window-shopping?"

Bel and Claire looked at each other, hesitating.

"Well, I don't suppose we'll be more than an hour in the museum, but you never know. We might easily get interested and want a bit longer. So you go to the Burger Bar when you are ready, and if we're not there yet, either wait for us, or come to the museum and find us there. You know where it is? Down Ample Street, next to the building with the dome."

"I know where it is," said Claire. "Don't let him bully you, Kate. You don't have to read out all the labels to him. He's quite capable of reading them himself."

Mum waved, and she and Paul moved away. They heard him saying, "It's just that I find it easier to take in the information if someone else reads it out to me. But I can help with the technical words if they're difficult for you."

Bel and Claire grinned at each other and looked around them. "*Young Ones* first?" Claire suggested.

They dived into the nearest shop and admired the clothes.

"I think I'll try this on," said Claire, lifting a hanger off the rail.

"I thought you didn't have any money with you?" Bel asked.

"Shut up," hissed Claire. "Do you think it's my

66

colour? Oh, look, they've got it in green. Why don't you try that one on?"

"I can't," Bel giggled.

"Of course you can. You just get a number from that woman at the till."

Claire marched up to the till, collected a plastic number, and strode off to the fitting room, smiling at Bel over her shoulder. Reluctantly Bel picked something from the rail, fetched a number, and followed her. An older girl was in the changing room trying on several different shirts and spinning round looking at herself in all the mirrors. Bel and Claire changed quickly and said nothing until she had left.

"I don't know why you do this for fun," said Bel. "You're always complaining about having to undress in public for PE at school."

"I like trying on different things. What on earth did you pick that for?"

"I thought it was rather elegant," said Bel, struggling to do up the zip down her back. "Give us a hand. How on earth do disabled people manage to dress themselves?"

"They have someone to do it for them," said Claire shortly. "This is too long for me. Pity, I quite like it otherwise."

"It must be horrible having to be dressed by someone else," said Bel. "Waiting for someone to put things on you. And if you're like Sarah, you can't even choose what you wear."

Some young women had come in with dresses over their arms. "No, I don't think this suits me," said Bel quickly.

"You might as well look at it properly," said Claire, "now that you've put it on. Here, I'll do the zip. It's not bad, actually."

"Undo it," said Bel. "I want to take it off." Claire laughed at her.

67

Bel tried stretching her arm down over her shoulder, then up from her waist. She could not reach the zip. "Don't be mean," she whispered, embarrassed in front of the other women. Claire had slipped her own clothes back on and was hovering by the curtained doorway. Bel thought she might go without her, leaving her zipped into the shop's dress.

"Shall I give you a hand?" one of the women asked, and in less than a second had undone the zip.

Bel thanked her, then left the changing room in silence and handed back the dress and the number. "That was horrible," she said to Claire.

"I was going to undo it," said Claire. "You didn't need to get upset about it. Anyway, I thought you'd like to know what it's like to be Sarah."

"Leave her alone!" said Bel angrily.

"Me!" said Claire. "It's you that talks about her all the time. Can't you just forget about her for a bit?"

Bel said nothing.

"Let's go in the Southgate Centre," said Claire. "We could look at some of the shoes. And there's the fancy knickers shop."

"I'm not trying anything else on," said Bel. "I don't trust you."

"They don't let you try on knickers anyway," said Claire. "Come on."

They looked at the frilly knickers and Claire tried on a lot of different shoes, just the left one of each pair that was out on display. Bel was relieved that she did not ask the assistant to fetch any from the stockroom. Then they moved on to *I'll Eat My Hat* and the stationery shop. Bel looked at some big plastic covers that could be slipped over a large sheet of paper and pinned to the wall.

"How big are these, do you think?" she asked Claire. "Ordinary paper is A4, so twice as big is A3. These must be A2. They'd be quite good." She was thinking that if Sarah used her charts a lot, they might get tatty. A plastic sleeve for them would be ideal. "Two pounds fifty! That's a lot."

"What would you use them for?" said Claire. She did not wait for an answer. "Look at these gold pens." She drew a flower on the back of her hand with one of them.

"They'll see you!" said Bel. "Stop it!"

"How can I know whether I want one if I don't try them out?" said Claire. She drew some silver leaves beside the golden flower.

"Come on," said Bel. "Let's go into the covered market. We can have a look at the bags."

"All right," said Claire. "There's a shop in there that sells Italian mugs. I know my mum likes them. I might get her one for her birthday. I'll see how much they are."

As they crossed the road to the market, a woman crossed the other way pushing a young man in a wheelchair. His arms were bent up so that his hands hung under his chin, and his head was pulled back and sideways.

"For God's sake!" said Claire, when they reached the far pavement. "Do you have to grin at people like that? Let's hope the man doesn't have any more brain than Sarah, or he'll think you're a right ninny, looking at him like that."

Bel thought she had just looked friendly. It was hard to get the right look. She hadn't wanted to avert her eyes as though the man was an ugly horror to be avoided, but perhaps such a bright smile was going a bit too far. You don't normally smile at complete strangers crossing the road.

After wandering up and down the avenues of the covered market they looked in the Burger Bar but Mum and Paul were not there yet.

"Shall we wait here for them?" Bel asked.

"It's a bit full," said Claire. "They won't want us hanging around without buying anything. Let's go and drag them out of the museum. Your poor mum will have had enough of it by now."

The museum was in a large old house with iron gates, and wide steps leading up to the door. If Bel had ever noticed it she had thought it was just another university building. A woman sitting at a table by the entrance looked searchingly at them, and sat up straighter.

"This is fantastic!" Bel said. The room they were in was crowded with glass cases, full of shining brass.

"Haven't you been here before?" said Claire. "I think it's a bit boring, actually. All these old compasses and sundials and things."

Bel tried reading a few of the labels. "I don't think I am very interested in finding out about them," she admitted. "But they look beautiful. What's that enormous thing that Paul's looking at?"

A great dark octagonal wooden tube was fixed in a stand, slanting up towards the ceiling.

"Come and see this," Mum said. "Paul's explaining what a mistake Newton made when he confused theoretical – what was it, Paul?"

"You can't see much through it," said Paul.

"Have you finished, then?" said Claire.

"There are some lovely globes upstairs, Bel," said Mum. "Pocket-sized. And just have a look at those grandfather clocks on the stairs. I've always fancied a grandfather clock."

"I'll sneak one out for you," said Bel. She went to the foot of the stairs and looked up to the landing. "They are nice. But a bit big for our hall, I think."

Claire had got Paul to the door. Mum and Bel followed them down the stone steps to the pavement, where Paul stopped to read the Latin inscription carved in a slab on the ground. Then they went on to the Burger Bar, where Paul embarrassed Mum by complaining about the fat level in the chips.

On the bus home, Bel remembered with a sinking heart that she had not tidied away her charts. There was not much hope that Claire would fail to notice them piled on the desk. She wondered whether she could pretend that they were some kind of homework, but Claire had all the same homework as her, except for French and Maths where she was in a higher group, and the charts were obviously for neither of those subjects. Perhaps she could keep Claire in the kitchen.

When they got home, she offered Claire a glass of orange, because Claire did not drink tea. "I'm not really thirsty, thanks," Claire said. "Do you want any help with tea, Kate?"

"No thanks, Claire," said Bel's mum. "It only needs heating up. Paul and I thought we'd have a game of Scrabble. Could you fetch the board for us, Bel? I think it's at the top of your wardrobe."

Bel hurried to the bedroom, scooped up the charts and shoved them on to the shelf in the wardrobe before pulling out the Scrabble box. Gilly was not there to ask questions. She must be out somewhere with Godfrey.

"Shall we play?" Claire asked when she brought it into the kitchen. "You any good at it?"

"Not really," said Bel. "I wanted to ask you about some of that geography. I can't remember how those air currents and things work, all that stuff about the temperature in continents."

"Oh, all right," said Claire unenthusiastically. She followed Bel to the bedroom and looked at Bel's maps of Asia and Australia.

"You've put the arrows in wrong," she said.

Suddenly there was a slithering noise from the wardrobe and the door burst open. Bel ignored it and carried on asking about the maps. "What's all that stuff you had in your wardrobe?" Claire asked. "You been drawing pictures?"

"Oh, it's something I did ages ago," said Bel. "It's nothing. So what are the green arrows supposed to be, anyway? I just copied them down and I forgot to see what they were."

Claire had picked up one of the sheets. "Floor, lap, wheelchair. What's this, roulette for Sarah so she can win a sit on your lap?" She looked at Bel. "It is for Sarah, isn't it? God, Bel, you're crazy. You think you can teach her to read from these coloured-in things?"

"It's not to teach her to read," Bel mumbled. "There's the pictures as well. It's just to give her a chance to choose things for herself."

"And what's Mrs Hinksey going to say to that?" demanded Claire.

"I thought I'd go and see her at the home where she lives," said Bel. "Just to see whether she can point to the things she wants to do. I know you think it's stupid."

"Well, its obviously a waste of time," said Claire, "but if that doesn't bother you, it doesn't bother me. When are you going to this home, then?"

"I haven't fixed it up yet," said Bel. "Maybe next Saturday. I'll have to ring."

"So you won't be coming to Cornhill with us, then? That's a shame, Dad said you could come. But I suppose you find Sarah's better company, really. Two people with no brain, you go together."

Bel knew that Cornhill meant a visit to Mrs Turnbull, a friend of Claire's father's who lived in a huge house with peacocks in the garden. Claire had told her about Mrs Turnbull's amazing collection of fossils, her illuminated manuscripts, and the enormous model railway layout in the attic. Bel could have visited Sarah in the morning, and still have gone to

Cornhill, but now it seemed that the invitation was withdrawn.

"What do you mean, no brain?" she asked. She felt she should be defending Sarah's brain, but was more upset about her own.

"Well, you can't manage your homework on your own, can you? I don't know how you managed to escape being sent to a special school yourself." Claire had always helped Bel with her homework, and had never seemed to mind. Sometimes Bel had helped her too, with ideas for English, or writing out lists for Claire to learn things from. Bel's writing was much clearer than Claire's. Bel suddenly saw into the bleak future. Even if Claire took her words back, apologised, said that she had never meant it, they could never be the same. How could Bel ever ask her advice again, even on the smallest thing, after this?

Bel closed her geography book and put it on the desk.

"It's all right," said Claire impatiently. "I'll tell you where the arrows go."

But Bel felt tears coming. She got up and went and shut herself in the bathroom. There she clenched her jaw until the tears had withdrawn again, flushed the toilet and came out to find Claire in the kitchen with Mum and Paul.

"So you've come to play after all?" said Mum. "Well, you haven't missed much as far as I'm concerned. I scored fourteen for my first word, and Paul used up his letters and got eighty-six. I think he should only be allowed four letters at a time."

"It was partly luck," said Paul. "I just happened to have a U to go with the Q."

Claire sat down and took seven letters. She groaned. "Come on, Bel," she said. "Let's see if we can't catch up with Paul."

But of course it was hopeless to try and catch up.

12   Willowbank and Snowdrop House

On Monday morning at school Bel and Claire pretended that nothing had changed. Bel still enjoyed
being with Claire. It was nice to sit next to a friend
and sometimes whisper during lessons, and to have
someone to talk to at break. But it was hard to keep
off the subject of Sarah, and now school work was a
touchy subject as well. Bel could agree when Claire
complained that a lesson had been boring, but dared
not say anything about the work they had done.

On the Wednesday, a theatre group came to Willowbank School to put on a show about road safety. They
did it in the school hall, acting in the middle of the
floor with all but the youngest children sitting in a
ring all round them. Bel and Claire's job was to sit
with some of the more fidgety children and try to keep
their attention on the show. Bel was relieved that
Mrs Hinksey had taken charge of Sylvia. With Mrs
Hinksey's hand lightly on her shoulder, Sylvia would
not move, but Bel's hand had no effect on her. She
had tried. Bel's fidgety little boy soon climbed on to
her lap, and sat quietly watching while he gently took
handfuls of the skin on her neck and stretched and
twisted it. It was uncomfortable, but not really pain-
ful, and Bel decided that it was worth putting up with
it, if it kept him quiet. Now and then she pointed out
what was happening in the show, or whispered to
him. She was not sure whether he was really noticing
at all what was going on.

Sarah was parked in her buggy near the door. Once or twice when the actors made the whole school roar with laughter Bel glanced over to see how she was reacting. But Sarah simply sat, drooping, in her chair, and did not seem even to be watching. Several times the actors asked for helpers from the audience, and all the children clamoured to be chosen, but Sarah made no movement. Claire had to cling on to the two children nearest her to stop them running straight on before they were chosen. Bel admired the way the actors chose not only the wildest and noisiest children, and managed to get them to play their parts, but also some very quiet shy ones. Joe was picked to be a lollipop man. He held his STOP sign up proudly and came back to his place beaming.

Towards the end of the show, when the children were beginning to get restless, the actors demanded a naughty child. Hands went up, though the older children carefully kept theirs in their laps, not wanting to label themselves naughty.

"No," said the woman actor who was in a police uniform. "I don't see any naughty children here at all. You only have good children at your school, Miss Wastie, do you? Ah, I think I can see just one! You at the back there, can you come out and help us, please? Yes, you. No, you."

It was Mrs Hinksey. The children giggled, and Mrs Hinksey, smiling with half her mouth, stepped carefully through the seated children and joined the actors in the middle of the room.

They wanted her to do all the things they had been warning against. Mrs Hinksey obediently crossed the road in dangerous places and ran out in front of moving cars. The children loved it. When a huge cardboard lorry with two of the actors inside it finally crashed into her, a roar of horror and delight went up. Bel glanced round at Sarah. At last she was enjoying herself. As Mrs Hinksey swung back on crutches to her place beside Sylvia, with a turban of bandages on her head, Sarah leaned back in her chair looking thoroughly satisfied.

Bel decided that tonight was the night to ring Snowdrop House. It was easy to chat to Claire on the way back to school about the show, and Mrs Hinksey's performance, and the different children's reactions, but in her head she was rehearsing the telephone conversation.

Sarah was being washed when the telephone rang. Sometimes Mrs Eaton and Davina gave her a bath, but she was heavy for them to lift in and out, and one of them had to kneel beside the bath the whole time to hold her shoulders and head out of the water. They did not do it very often. Sarah did not like being washed. She had to lie on a towel on a table. It was too high up, and she got cold.

"You are a good girl, Sarah," Mrs Eaton was saying. "Now your feet. There we are, all nice and clean. Oh, drat it, there's the telephone. What can they be thinking of, ringing just when we're getting them all ready for bed? Davina! Can you answer it?"

The telephone went on ringing. Mrs Eaton went as close to the door as she could without taking one hand off Sarah's shoulder, ready to catch her if she should move suddenly and look like falling off the table.

"Davina! Will you get the phone, please!"

The ringing stopped. Mrs Eaton wrapped the towel round Sarah, braced herself to lift her, and then carried her over to a mat on the floor where she could safely get her dressed.

"Ooh, we've got our new pyjamas to put on today, Sarah, the ones your mummy sent you. Aren't they lovely? Who's this on the front, eh?" She held up the pyjama top for Sarah to see.

Donald Duck! Sarah shouted. Her mother had

chosen the pyjamas because Sarah used to laugh when she talked in a Donald Duck voice. She had sent a dressing gown too, blue like her own.

"That's Donald Duck, Sarah."

Davina came into the bathroom leading Timothy by the hand. "Let's run your bath, Tim. Are you going to get in with Joe today and play nicely? No splashing like yesterday?"

"Not me splash," said Timothy. "Joe splash. Joe take my fish."

Davina rummaged among the bath toys. "Here, now, there's two fish. One for you, one for Joe. So no fighting today, all right?" The water gushed out of the taps and steam covered the window.

"Who was that on the phone, Davina?" Mrs Eaton asked.

"Oh, yes, I forgot," said Davina. "Somebody wanting to come and visit Sarah at the weekend. A visitor for you, Sarie! How about that?"

"A relative?" asked Mrs Eaton.

"No, just a schoolgirl. I can't remember her first name. Taphouse was the surname. She said she's been helping at Willowbank, and she'd like to come and see Sarah. I told her she'd have to ring at the weekend to check with the weekend staff, in case they're going out at all. Not that they're likely to take Sarah out on any trips. You're off this weekend, aren't you?"

"Yes," said Mrs Eaton. "It's my nephew's wedding on Saturday."

"Oh, yes! Of course it is! Come on, then, Timmy, you can get it off if you pull a bit harder. That's right. Now your vest. Did you get your skirt finished yet?"

"Nearly," answered Mrs Eaton, heaving Sarah up to a sitting position while she threaded her arms into the sleeves of the new blue dressing gown. "You can run upstairs and have a look at it when you come off

77

duty. I've only got the hem to take up. I do think it's a bit, you know, but it's not often you get a chance to wear that sort of thing."

"Oh no, it'll be lovely. I hope the weather holds out for them. Where's the reception? Is it going to be big?"

"About two hundred. They've hired some room, I can't remember what they called it. Six bridesmaids, would you believe, and mostly little ones. I told my brother, I said six, you must be mad. All the dresses, and of course anything can happen."

"Oh, it'll be smashing. Now, Timmy, let me feel the water first. Yes, that's all right. Can you keep an eye on him, Mrs Eaton while I fetch Joe? In you jump, then, Tim."

Now Mrs Eaton laid Sarah down again and buttoned the dressing gown.

"Oh, aren't we smart, Sarah!" said Davina when she came back, leading Joe. "Look, Joe, Sarah's got a new dressing gown!"

"Blue," said Joe, nervously. Bel had done a good job of teaching him his colours in the end.

"Mind you," said Davina thoughtfully. "It looks a bit more like a boy's one to me, that colour."

"Oh, I don't know," said Mrs Eaton. "I don't see why the girls shouldn't have a nice bright blue. It's lovely, isn't it, Sarah? And did you see her pyjamas? Donald Duck, aren't they, Sarah?"

"It's none too big for her, though, is it?" said Davina. "Those sleeves are only just long enough. Her mother doesn't realise how much she's grown, does she?"

"She is getting a bit taller," said Mrs Eaton. "Or longer, whichever way you like to put it. But it's a while since her mother's been down. She's got her own life to lead, I suppose, and it's not as though Sarah misses her or anything. Anyway, it will be nice if that schoolgirl wants to come and see her. Maybe

78

she'll take her out for a walk. You'd like that, wouldn't you, Sarah?"

Sarah was sure it was Isabel who was going to visit, and she knew why she was coming. To Sarah, Bel was a grown-up, no different from the other grown-ups who towered over her. Isabel had said once that she would find a way for her to talk. Sometimes Sarah had thought she had forgotten, but no, all the time she had been working on it. Last Wednesday she had been specially enthusiastic. She had told Sarah that she had something ready to help her to talk. She said she would bring it to Snowdrop House. Perhaps she had found a doctor who could make Sarah's voice work the way it was meant to, and was going to bring the medicine. Or perhaps she had a machine to plug into Sarah's mind and let all the thoughts out.

Isabel might have been studying disabled people somewhere else, so that now she would be able to understand what Sarah said. After all, Duncan could sometimes understand her, so why not a grown-up? Sarah had proved to Isabel herself that she knew what was what.

One day when they were waiting to go swimming, Isabel had shown Sarah some pairs of pictures, asking her to choose the one which answered a question. There were three pairs of pictures, and Sarah knew she had chosen the right answer each time. An umbrella and a balloon – which one keeps the rain off you? A banana and a fork – which one can you eat? A house and a tree – which one can you live in? Bel had done it secretly while Mrs Hinksey was out of the room, and then she had pushed the pictures back into her pocket and said, "There! I knew you could do it!" Now she would help her to prove it to everyone else. Sarah wondered whether Isabel could teach her to walk as well.

The weekend meant Saturday and Sunday. Sarah

hoped that Isabel would come on Saturday, then she could practise talking all Sunday and surprise them at school next week. She did not think she could wait until Sunday. She had waited all her life, and now the next few days seemed as long again.

"Stop kicking, now, Sarah," said Mrs Eaton as she carried her to the bedroom. "You'll make me drop you one of these days. You know, she must have put on quite a bit of weight since the summer, Davina. I know she's small for her age, but there's no way we'll be able to cope with her when she's eleven or twelve. Still, I suppose they'll find somewhere for her to go." She laid Sarah in her cot. "Do you want to face the window, then, Sarah? I'll leave the curtains open for a little while so's you can see out. Let's wind up your music box, shall we, then? You are a good girl!"

The music tinkled and a baby grumbled in the room across the passage where it was lying in its cot waiting to fall asleep. Joe and Timothy argued in the bath and Davina shouted at them for splashing water on the floor. The next pair of children was brought upstairs ready to be bathed. Everything was usual, except that Isabel was coming on Saturday to teach Sarah to talk. She felt like singing. She let out a great roar.

Mrs Eaton rushed back into the bedroom. "What is it? Sarah! You are not to make such a noise! Waking the babies, and giving us all a fright. Now, go to sleep." She pulled the curtains and switched out the light. Sarah obediently closed her eyes and tried to imagine what she would do with the new power of speech.

13 Snowdrop House

Bel was slightly dreading the visit to Snowdrop House. She had in her mind a picture of herself sitting on a lawn with Sarah, chatting to her in a relaxed way, with Sarah replying by pointing to words or sentences on cards spread out on the grass around them. Bel would read books to her, and begin her real education. She had even picked out a few old children's books from her own cupboard that they could look at together. But this was a picture, she thought, of some time in the future. What she imagined for this Saturday was the awkwardness of arriving at Snowdrop House, of not knowing which was the front door and whether to knock or ring or walk straight in.

It rained on Saturday morning, and anyway Mum wanted help with the housework, so it was lunch-time before Bel got round to ringing Snowdrop House. Someone different from last time answered, a man. "Hello, Snowdrop House, Terry speaking."

"Oh, hello, I'm Isabel Taphouse and I rang last Wednesday to see if it would be all right to come and visit Sarah. Would that be convenient, I mean it doesn't matter if it isn't, I can make it some other time if that would be better?"

"I'm sorry, who is this speaking?"

"Bel Taphouse," said Bel more slowly. "I wanted to come and see Sarah. Sarah Anscombe. Is she busy or anything?"

"Sarah? No, Sarah's not busy. Fine, are you coming this afternoon? OK, I'll put her down for a visitor. See you later."

When she had put the phone down, Bel realised that she did not know where Snowdrop House was. She did not like to ring back and ask the man she had just spoken to. It could not be far from the school, anyway. She looked it up in the telephone directory, and eventually found it listed under the name of the County Council. Now she knew the name of the road it was in, Sycamore Avenue.

"I'm going over to Gran's this afternoon," said Mum at lunch. "Do you want to come with me? You're not going over to Claire's father's, are you. Gran would love to see you."

"I can't," said Bel. "I've arranged to go and visit Sarah. You know, that little girl that I used to see at her school, the one who can't talk."

"Well, that's nice of you," said Mum. "I didn't know that you were planning to see them at the weekends as well. But don't go upsetting her. She's probably quite happy the way she is."

"You sound like Mrs Hinksey," said Bel. "She isn't happy the way she is. But I don't intend to upset her either."

"Is she nice?" Mum asked.

"What?" said Bel.

"Your little girl. Is she nice?"

Bel considered. "I like her. But I don't know if you would call her nice. I think that's what makes me think she must be intelligent. All the children are nice the way that little kids are, you know, funny sometimes, or sweet, or affectionate, but they don't seem like people, or not enough for you to like or dislike them or choose them as friends. But Sarah does seem like a person, not sweet or babyish. Maybe that's why Mrs Hinksey doesn't like her so much. You can't really tell whether she's nice or not. She doesn't have much opportunity to behave nicely or nastily."

"Hmm," said Mum. "So it would be interesting to get to know her. I don't know anything about handicapped people. I suppose I feel a bit nervous about them. But I wouldn't mind meeting this Sarah."

"I'd like you to, Mum," said Bel. "Maybe you would see what I mean about her. I think they have a fete at Snowdrop House later in the year. I saw a poster up at the school asking people to make suggestions for stalls. We could go to that, and you could meet some of the children."

"All right," said Mum. "If I'm feeling brave."

"You don't have to feel brave," said Bel scornfully. "They are just people like us, only with a few problems."

"It's all very well saying that," said Mum. "It's just not knowing exactly what sort of problems they have. And don't pretend you weren't nervous the first time you went to that school."

"A bit," Bel admitted. "But a fete is easy. You can pretend to be after bargains on the cake stall. You don't have to get involved. And I'll introduce you to the children."

Mum set off alone to visit Gran, and Bel got ready to walk to Snowdrop House. It was still raining. It would almost be possible to stay at home reading for the afternoon, and forget about Sarah. Although it was only three days since Bel had seen her, and only three more before they met again, she seemed to be part of a different life. Bel tried to judge how guilty she would feel if she broke her promise to visit Sarah again. Then, remembering Sarah's crooked grin, she noticed that, mixed in with nervousness at dealing with the Snowdrop House staff, she was looking forward to seeing her.

She rolled up her cards and sheets of paper and put

them, with a few books and her little collection of different sorts of food, in one carrier bag inside another. She thought of wearing her school uniform, to help Sarah remember her, but it was too much on a Saturday. She put on a black jumper that might look similar enough to her school one, put up the hood of her raincoat and wrinkled her face against the rain. It was not heavy.

She went to the school first. It was closed, of course. She would have felt embarrassed to meet Mrs Hinksey and have to explain that she was visiting Sarah and, in Mrs Hinksey's view, unsettling her. Bel wondered what Mrs Hinksey would be doing today. She had picked up nothing about her private life at all. In the classroom or on expeditions, all the talk had been about the children, or occasionally about research that had been done into mental handicap or education. Sylvia had a particularly interesting syndrome. Bel could never remember its name.

The school looked strange with the windows and doors all closed, no tricycles or wheelchairs in the playground, and the gates padlocked shut. There were puddles on the tarmac. The bright paint on the playground toys sparkled, glazed with rain water.

Sycamore Avenue was not any of the roads close by the school. Bel decided that she would have to ask someone where it was. Several likely people went hurrying past before she plucked up courage to ask them. A woman carrying two coats in plastic bags fresh from the cleaners, anxious to get them home before the rain got at them, pointed her in the right direction. It was not far at all.

Snowdrop House looked all right. Bel had imagined another square modern building like the school, surrounded by tarmac, but it looked like an ordinary house, though very large. Probably it had been built for a rich family a hundred years ago, who had to have enough space for all their servants. There was a tall clipped hedge in front, a neat round bed of rose bushes set in a narrow strip of lawn, and a heavy blue door with a ramp leading up to it. Bel could hear music coming from a half-open window, a shout from another. She rang the door-bell, and heard on the other side of the thick wood a high voice calling, "Lisa! Lisa! The door! Someone's at the door!"

Someone, Lisa, opened the door. She did not look much older than Gilly. And there was Duncan. It was Duncan who had called out. Bel had not realised how pleased she would be to see him and the other children again. All her thoughts had focussed on Sarah. Duncan was plump and ungainly, with hair that stuck straight out from his head like straw. Bel saw his smile again and felt like hugging him.

"Hello, Duncan! How are you?" Bel stepped inside and rubbed her feet hard on the mat. Her shoes were soaked.

"Don't worry about that," said the girl, Lisa. "We get all kinds of things on these floors."

"I've been swimming with Terry," said Duncan proudly. "And I took off all my own clothes myself. I was very a good boy. Terry said. Joe got his towel stuck down that thing."

He held on to Bel's hand and looked up into her face. It was strange that it was the little boy who was at ease and ready to make conversation about anything. Bel looked round the hall. It was not just an entrance passage. As well as a rack of hooks full of coats, there was a battered old sofa, and a small hutch under the wide, shallow stairs had something rustling in its straw.

"Come and see the television." Duncan pulled at her hand. "Not on till five o'clock. Come and see it."

Bel resisted the pull, and said to Lisa, "I've really come to see Sarah. Is she around?"

"Oh, yes," said the girl. "She's in the hobbies room. Duncan, show the lady the hobbies room, will you?"

"Not a lady," said Duncan. "That's Isabel. She's a teacher at my school."

The girl looked disbelieving, but did not wait for an explanation. Bel followed Duncan along a passage, down a ramp and through a glass door. Duncan pushed against the door with all his might and managed to squeeze his way through. Sarah was in her buggy, parked by an empty table, waiting for Bel. The room was bare, with a stained vinyl floor and several formica-topped tables. There were windows in three of the walls, and low cupboards ran all round the room. Childish paintings were pinned up between the windows, and mobiles made from milk-bottle-tops and yogurt cartons hung from the ceiling.

Bel felt shy.

"Here's Isabel come to see you, Sarah," said Duncan. "Shall I move you?" He bent to take the brake off the buggy, but Sarah kicked and shouted and he jumped up, looking scared.

"Sarah's always cross with me," he said, looking as though he might cry.

Sarah made a noise.

"You are," said Duncan. "I'm always helping you, and you're always cross."

Sarah made another noise and Duncan laughed. Then someone called to him from the passage and he clumsily pulled the glass door open again, getting his feet in the way, and ran plodding out.

"Hello, Sarah," said Bel. "It's nice to see you at home for a change." She wondered whether Sarah thought of this place as home. If she thought at all. Well, of course she could think. Hadn't she pointed to the right one of all Bel's sets of pictures?

I've been waiting all day, said Sarah, and watched her face. But it was no good, she could see from

86

Isabel's face that she had not learnt to understand her. She waited for Isabel to say how she was going to talk.

"I couldn't come earlier," said Bel, "because my mother wanted me to clean the bathroom and do loads of tidying up. I'll put my coat on this chair. I've brought some things to show you."

She can't have forgotten about helping me to talk, thought Sarah. She accused her of it out loud. Usually she did not bother to talk to adults. They ignored her, or told her to stop making those horrible noises. But she would make Isabel listen to her.

"Have you had a nice morning?" Bel asked. Sarah's eyes turned to the window and Bel followed her gaze.

"Raining? It's raining too much! Yes, it is!"

At last! Maybe she had learnt something.

"I brought some things," said Bel, unfolding the plastic bags. The paper inside was damp and some of the ink had run. "Oh dear, it's all wet. You see, I brought things you could point at, to show what you want to say. If we work it out right, I think you could say almost anything."

Sarah looked at the curled sheets of paper, smudged with colours and bent from being rolled up for too long. Isabel was looking proud but anxious. Sarah felt that she had never met anyone as stupid as her. Was this what she meant by talking? Some sheets of paper? It couldn't be. Sarah must have got it wrong. In a minute Isabel would tell her the real news, about something that a doctor could do to her mouth to make it talk.

Bel spread the sheets out on the table. She was glad that there was nobody else in the room, because she felt unsure of herself. "See these colours? Whichever you choose means you want something on the big circle that's the same colour. So if you choose orange, I'll get you the orange circle and you can choose something on there. That's games and toys. Or if you chose yellow, then you could pick something to drink off the yellow circle. Or you could use the green circle to ask me to change what position you are in. Do you see?"

Bel expected the jerk of the head that Sarah had used for 'yes' at school. Instead her head hung heavily down on her chest. Bel's heart sank. Could Mrs Hinksey have been right? "Please try, Sarah," said Bel. "I know it doesn't look that brilliant, with the smudges and everything, but it's a beginning, isn't it? Shall I explain again?"

Sarah's head moved, but not in any way that seemed to Bel to mean anything. Then Sarah swept the papers to one side and shouted with anger. She kicked her legs and banged on the table. She wanted to talk, not to point to stupid things that someone else had chosen to colour on bits of stupid paper.

"Oh, never mind," said Bel, and gathered up the sheets of paper. It looked as though they would be no use. "It was just an idea. I've brought some books. Would you like me to read you a story?"

Grudgingly Sarah pulled her head back. She could not understand what had happened to the plans to teach her to talk, and tears fell from her eyes, but she did not want Isabel to leave. Bel had brought clean tissues on purpose, knowing that Sarah was likely to dribble or cry. Sarah let Bel wipe her cheeks and nose, and let her read the story.

"So then the mice had a nice new house," Bel finished. "They deserved it, after all that, didn't they? Did you like that book?" She knew as she asked that it was unfair to ask such question of someone who could only say 'yes'.

"I'm sorry, Sarah," she said quickly. "It's awful. I'm useless. But there must be some way for you to say things." So she had done nothing about helping Sarah to talk except make those stupid bits of paper. Sarah groaned.

"While we're working on it, is there anything I could do for you?" Bel felt helpless. For some reason Sarah did not want to use the carefully drawn circles. She wondered if they could have been any good. Perhaps Sarah was not capable anyway of movements exact enough to point to one of six choices. There must be something she could do.

Sarah pointed to the book with her eyes. Without realising that it was Sarah who had directed her attention to it, Bel picked it up from the table. "Would you like me to read it again?" she asked carefully.

Sarah swung away, then turned her eyes to it again. *I want to read it, you idiot. Can't you teach me to read? Fool, stupid fool.*

Bel knew that Sarah was angry. What could she do? She opened the book at the first page. "The mouse family had nowhere to live," she began. Sarah interrupted her. *The mouse family had nowhere to live.*

The sounds meant nothing, but Bel recognised the rhythm of the sentence, slowed and distorted. She looked up at Sarah. Still she was not confident of her intelligence. It sounded to her almost the kind of thing that a baby would say, mimicking the outline of a phrase, but unable to copy the exact sounds or the sense. Sarah saw the doubt in Isabel's face.

Reluctantly, not wanting to be caught doing anything foolish, Bel pointed to the words, holding the book so that Sarah could see the page easily. She read the whole book slowly aloud, pointing to each word with her finger. At the same time she was turning over in her mind ideas about how Sarah could learn to read. Should she learn the alphabet? Bel remembered the plastic letters that Mum had used to teach Gilly and her.

It was not Sarah's first reading lesson. She watched

television, and knew the names of the different break-fast cereals, car names, brands of margarine from the advertisements. She had seen all the words that Mrs Hinksey stuck up around the classroom, and she had heard her teaching David and Duncan their letters. "Start at the top, then down, up and around" or "Top to bottom, then up and over" as she tried to guide their thick pencils. Sarah could not see the shapes they were making, but she listened and imagined. Her good right hand, the one that only existed in her mind, could hold an invisible pencil and make the shapes for her, perfectly formed, not like the sprawling efforts of the other children in the class. She leant forward, never taking her eyes from the page.

"Is that what you wanted?" Bel asked. "You want to read?" Sarah nodded, yes.

"Is that book too easy?" A toss of the head, no.

"I'll bring some other books next week. Once you've learnt to read ..." but Bel stopped herself from making any promises. She imagined Sarah revealed as having normal intelligence, perhaps a genius. She wouldn't stay at Snowdrop House, of course. It was only for mentally handicapped children. Bel thought of the staff here, and the teachers at the school, as jailers, conspiring with Sarah's stubborn arms and legs to keep her imprisoned.

Some of the bigger children burst in. Terry had promised them that they could do painting, as it was too wet to go out.

"Hello, there," said Terry to Bel, following the children in. He was not much older than Lisa, yet some of the children were Bel's own age or older. She thought it must be a strange job for the two of them.

"Hello," said Bel. "I was reading to Sarah." She pushed the book into her bag almost guiltily.

"That's nice," said Terry. Bel could not tell whether he thought she was ridiculous.

"Are you going to stay and watch the painting, Sarah?" she asked.

Sarah looked towards the door.

"OK, you show me where you want to go," said Bel. "Is that all right?" she asked Terry.

"Fine, you can take her anywhere downstairs." Terry crouched down by a cupboard to get out jars of paint and brushes. Bel pulled open the door and pushed Sarah through. At the end of the corridor she walked round to face her and asked her which way to go. Following Sarah's directions, they ended up in the kitchen. Here Sarah was clearly asking for food.

"I don't know if I'm allowed to get you food," she said awkwardly.

"No," said a large pale girl in thick glasses, taller than Bel, who had wandered in after them. "Only allowed food at tea-time. No, Sarah, no food."

The whole thing was useless. Sarah roared with despair. Lisa came and took her away for a rest, and thanked Bel for visiting. Sarah cried in the office, darkened with the curtains pulled, and Bel cried as she walked home, thinking that no-one would notice because of the rain. She took the chocolate out of her bag and ate it hurriedly, then the cheese, then the marmite sandwich, the peanut butter sandwich and the banana, which was squashed, all the time pretending to herself that she was not eating them, and that preparing them had not been a waste of time.

Mum and Gilly were both out when she arrived home. She tore up the sheets of coloured paper and read angrily through all her old children's books. One thing had come out of the afternoon. She no longer felt any need to test Sarah, or prove again to herself that Sarah understood things. Her anger and frustration had been too obvious. Bel still wanted to help Sarah, but she felt frustrated too, and resented her anger. Surely she should be grateful to Bel for trying to help. Then she felt guilty, because she should be happy to help without expecting gratitude. Her feelings curdled uncomfortably inside her.

Usually Bel found the old familiar books soothing, but today the words jangled in front of her eyes and the pictures seemed to be taunting her.

She heard Mum come in. Soon there was a smell of bread toasting and she knew that in a little while she would allow herself to be cheered up by it. She kicked the bed-leg and thought how much easier other people's lives were compared to hers. The rabbits on the open page on her lap seemed to be jeering at her with their simple pleasures.

"What's up, Bel?" Mum had come into the room. Bel realised that she had been knocking on the door for some time.

Bel snapped the book shut and put it on the desk face down. Mum smiled a little, thinking it sweet that Bel should go back to her babyhood and read the old books now and then.

"Come and have some tea, love?"

"Mm, all right."

"What's all that stuff in the bin?" Mum asked, before she remembered that it was none of her business and that Bel was entitled to her privacy. Anyway she could probably have a glance through it on dustbin day if it looked really interesting.

Bel felt like crying again, mostly because her eyes had got into the habit during the afternoon. It would take a night's sleep for them to recover. She thought one of the worst things about crying is that your eyes are so uncontrollable for the rest of the day.

"Didn't your visit go well, then, love?" Mum sat down on the edge of the bed, and put her arm along the back of Bel's chair, feeling that putting it actually on Bel's shoulders might be resented.

"It's so horrible for her!" said Bel. "It's like being

trapped. She can't do anything. I feel so sorry for her, but I don't know how to help her." She did feel sorry for Sarah, but just now she was feeling as well that Sarah should be making more effort to be helped.

"Are you really sure you're right about her?" Mum asked seriously.

Bel sniffed and swallowed and moved away from the edge of tears. "There's no doubt at all," she answered, looking straight at Mum. "She was angry today because I couldn't help her. But she was telling me what she wanted. And she can tell you things by the way she looks. I didn't notice it before. She looked at the rain to tell me that it had been raining all morning. Really, Mum, she isn't stupid."

"Well," said Mum briskly. "It's about time you told someone about it." She stood up and picked up Bel's nightie from the floor, shook it out and folded it, slipped it under the pillow and straightened the cover.

Bel felt indignant. "What do you mean, tell someone? They won't believe me!"

"Oh, come on, love," said Mum. "You did sort of tell her teacher, but you can't blame her for not taking any notice. I mean, you were messing about in her classroom, doing things she hadn't asked you to do and probably causing a lot of trouble."

"I wasn't," said Bel sullenly, but she knew that this was not the important part of the conversation.

"You need to get in touch with the expert, whoever it is that assesses the kids, and explain why you think Sarah should be tested again. She should be in a proper school for physically handicapped people, where they have all these electronic gadgets and things, if her brain works all right."

"They couldn't help her in a school," said Bel stupidly. She felt that she was the only person able to defend Sarah from the hard world. She hadn't

93

succeeded so far, but she cared enough about her to find a way for her to talk. "I'll think of a way to help her."

"Look, she's not a pet," said Mum. "If you're right, it must be hell for her, being treated like a baby. If you won't tell the person who's responsible, I will."

"How are you going to find out who it is that tests them?" asked Bel, almost jeering. "It's an educational psychologist that goes round to lots of different schools. You can't just ring the school and ask to speak to her."

Mum sighed. "Come on, Bel, you don't own her, you know. The best way to help her is to get the experts on to her. They'll know what to do. There must be other people like her."

"You'll get me into trouble, Mum," said Bel. "I can't tell anyone anything until I've finished the community project. The psychologist would be sure to say why she was testing Sarah, and Mrs Hinksey would go mad, and I'd get into trouble with Miss Radcot, and I wouldn't get my certificate. You wanted me to get my certificate, didn't you?"

"All right, don't panic," said Mum. "The child's waited, how old is she?"

"Nine, I think, or eight."

"She's waited nine years, she can wait another few weeks till the end of term. Then you can swing into action."

"I'll go and see her again next weekend," said Bel. "Maybe I can help a bit."

They went into the kitchen, putting aside for the moment the question of finding the educational psychologist, and persuading her that Sarah was worth more attention.

14 Snowdrop House

Sarah did not know that Isabel had promised herself that she would visit her every Saturday. She had not come into the classroom on Wednesday to help with the baking. Perhaps she would never come again, since Sarah had been so angry with her. Sarah was not sure whether she cared or not. Then she remembered how Isabel had helped her to join in all the different things that the class did on Wednesdays, and she cared very much.

The following weekend Bel found her in her cot. They were short-staffed. Sarah had been put to bed for an afternoon rest and no-one had got her up again. There was no answer when Bel rang the door-bell so she let herself in. The children in the television room told her that Sarah was upstairs. She looked into each of the big bedrooms. They were tidy, but she was warmed by the signs of the children's lives and personalities, toys on the pillows, posters over the beds, and stickers on the locker doors. The strangeness of finding Sarah in bed cut across Bel's awkwardness at seeing her again.

"Do you want to get up?" she asked. "Shall I ask if I can get you up?"

Yes. Yes.

"Wait a minute. I'll go and ask Terry if that's all right."

Hurry up then, I'm sick of lying here, and it will be bed-time again in a few hours.

Bel ran downstairs to find Terry. Through the window she saw him on the lawn with a group of children, playing catch with a large soft ball. She felt shy at the thought of interrupting the game. Then she heard a noise in the kitchen. Lisa was spooning food into two large babies strapped into high chairs. Bel wondered whether it was a late lunch or early tea.

"Can I get Sarah up and bring her downstairs?" she asked.

"Oh God, is she still in bed?" said Lisa vaguely. "Yes, do. You know how to work the lift?"

"No, but Sarah can show me," said Bel casually, not noticing the effect of this statement on Lisa, who spooned a blob of food into one of the children's necks.

Bel was very careful with Sarah. She asked whether she wanted her shoes on. Sarah said no, she would prefer slippers. She only wore shoes to school. Bel asked for advice on how to lift her into the buggy. Holding her under the arms? Yes. Were the straps comfortable? No. It was going well. Bel felt that she had been so rude to Sarah up till now, picking her up, putting her down, never waiting for her to answer. Sarah still could not say a word, but watching her Bel could work out what she wanted, if it was not too complicated.

"You'll have to show me the lift," she said. "I don't even know where it is." She watched Sarah's eyes and was led easily to the lift. It had only two buttons, for up and down, but she checked with Sarah first out of politeness.

"Where shall we go?" Bel asked. "Don't take me anywhere that we're not supposed to go. I don't want us to get into trouble."

They went to the day-room again with all its windows. The sun was shining today and with the

96

radiators on full blast as well, the room was as hot as a green-house.

Open the window, said Sarah.

"The sun is shining?" said Bel.

The window.

"Shall I open the windows? All right, if I can find out how." Only the top windows opened, with cords. "What do you want to do today?" Bel asked.

The bag.

Bel had brought a carrier bag again, but Sarah knew that she would not have brought the coloured sheets of paper today.

"Shall I show you what I brought? Some books, some plastic alphabet letters, where are they? Yes, here. Some farm animals. Mum always puts one in my Christmas stocking. She gave me a family of piglets this year. I still like them." Bel stopped to wonder whether Sarah ever had a Christmas stocking. Would she have gone home to her parents' house for Christmas, or would Terry and Lisa cook a Christmas dinner and mash it up for Sarah to eat? She dug down to the bottom of the bag. "Here's some toy cars that I had. Oh, yes, and some chocolate buttons. Are you allowed to eat those?"

Sarah fixed her gaze on the chocolate, and Bel shyly fed them to her, one by one. She did not chew them, but they disappeared and she only dribbled a little. Sometimes Bel took one for herself, and Sarah would protest, kicking and shouting, but with a big grin on her face.

"I'm a pig, aren't I?"

Sarah agreed, delighted. Now I'd like to look at the cars.

"Here, this one is an old-fashioned car."

Yes, I know, it's a Rolls Royce.

"They usually have the names underneath. Let's see. Oh yes, it's a Rolls Royce. And this one is a Ford

Capri. Look, the boot opens and shuts. And this is a Renault Five, and here's a mini. The mini has three doors that really open, and look, you can see the steering wheel and the hand-brake inside. It's good, isn't it?"

Bel lined the cars up on the table beside Sarah. She had never played much with cars as a child and was not sure what she should do with them.

Can I keep them? Sarah asked. She looked towards the door, and the ceiling.

"The light? The light's off, yes, we don't need it with the sun shining in. What, the ceiling? The door? Upstairs? You want to go upstairs? The cars upstairs? Shall we take the cars upstairs? All right, if you want to. No? Later on, then. Oh, yes, of course, you can take them upstairs. You can keep them by your bed if you like. I don't need them any more."

Bel felt worn out at the effort of understanding, but made herself remember that Sarah must be even more tired out by having to make her understand. She sat back and smiled at Sarah. But Sarah did not want a rest. She was looking at the other things Bel had taken from her bag.

"Do you want to look at the letters now?" She opened the box and took out some of the letters. "Do you know the letters? Do you know what sounds they make?"

Most of them, I think.

Bel looked doubtful. "Shall I tell you?"

Yes.

"I'll show you the simple ones first. Some letters make all different sounds depending what else they're with. But look, this is your letter, S. It's always suh. Well, no, sometimes it's zzz, but mostly suh. And this is B, buh for Bel."

Bel? I thought you were called Isabel.

"Me? Yes, that's B for Bel. Oh, yes, my real name's

Isabel, but most people call me Bel. Just at school I'm called Isabel. You can call me Bel. Is there anything you like being called?"

No, just Sarah. Definitely not Sarie.

The letters were spread out on the table, wide apart so that Sarah could choose them with her gaze. She chose B, and Bel put it on the edge of the table close by her. She chose S. It took a few guesses on Bel's part to work out which letter she wanted, but there was no doubt about it when they got the right one. Sarah pulled her head back further than ever before. B for Bel, S for Sarah. But it was too much to expect that Sarah would be able to spell whole words out.

"It's a bit hard with letters," said Bel. "I know, I'll cut up some bits of paper and write whole words on them. We'll see if that's any use. I suppose I can use some of this paper, can't I?" She found a pile of flimsy white paper in one of the cupboards and tore it into rectangles as neatly as she could.

"I'll write our names, Bel, Sarah. I wonder what other words we could use?" She wrote and read out, "'Sarah lives in Bishopcross'. Look, I can change it if I take out 'Sarah'. Now it says 'Bel lives in Bishopcross'."

Bel pushed the letters to one side and spread the words out on the table. With only five pieces of paper, widely scattered, it should be easier to be sure which one Sarah was indicating.

"Which one says 'Bishopcross', Sarah?"

Sarah leaned, looked and pointed. There was no doubt that she knew which word was 'Bishopcross'.

"Which one says 'in'?"

This time Sarah just stared at the word, and tilted a little towards it. Pointing was hard work.

"You are clever! Shall I write some more words?"

Sarah pulled back her head. She was hoping for so many words. She needed to say that she wanted her pocket money to be spent on a Leeds United shirt like Timothy's. She wanted Bel to write to her mother and tell her that she understood everything. She wanted to tell Bel about the children's money being taken by Mrs Churchill.

Bel wrote out 'hungry', 'thirsty', 'tired' and 'uncomfortable' so that Sarah could say how she was feeling. She wrote 'likes', and made the sentence 'Bel likes Sarah'. Then she took out some of the farm animals and wrote their names on scraps of paper.

"I'll put them by their own names," she said, standing the cow, the pig, the horse and the sheep by the right words. "Have a good look at them. Then I'll muddle the words up. Which animal does this word go with?"

It was 'pig'. Sarah looked hard at the little pink piece of plastic. She had seen pigs on television, and cows. She got all the words right.

"We'd better stop," said Bel. "You'll wear out. But I think you're brilliant. Most kids take ages to learn to read. You're really quick." She started to pack the paper and toys away into her bag. Sarah jumped in her buggy and shouted. Don't put them away.

"Do you want to look at them some more?"

Yes.

Bel spread the words out on the table again. "Shall I test you on them again?" she asked.

No.

They had not discussed how to say no, but it was obvious. Sarah would turn her face away, with a disgusted expression, and nobody who was wondering what she was thinking could have misunderstood. Bel wondered what Sarah was planning. She looked at her doubtfully. Sarah knew what she wanted to say. She pointed her eyes plainly at the word 'Bel'.

"Bel?" she checked, touching the word. "Is that the one you wanted? That's me."

Sarah moved her gaze to another word. Bel hesitated.

"Do you want me to tell you what it says? Are you testing me this time? It says 'pig'."

No, no, no.

"Yes, this says pig. Look, puh, ih, guh. Oh, sorry, try again."

Bel, pig. Bel, pig. Bel pig.

"Bel pig? What!" screamed Bel. She felt like crying. "Do you mean Bel is a pig?"

Yes.

"Just because I ate a tiny bit of your chocolate? You beast! You horrible, horrible girl!"

Sarah laughed until her whole body was shaking and her legs kicked up and down.

Bel was thrilled. She realised that until now she had not fully believed in Sarah, but had been waiting for this complete proof of her intelligence. She grabbed the handles of the buggy and danced round, spinning it on the smooth floor. Sarah leant back and shouted at the ceiling. They were delighted with themselves.

Suddenly the door opened, and two women came in, one in a bright apron with an elephant on the front, the other very tall and smartly dressed. Bel felt as though she and Sarah were small children, caught out behaving badly.

"Look who's here, Sarah," said Mrs Eaton. "Excuse me, Mrs Anscombe. I must get back to the others."

"Yes, of course, thank you," said Sarah's mother. "Hello, Sarah, how are you?"

She sat down near the buggy, ignoring Bel. She took one of Sarah's hands in hers and stared at her. Bel stood awkwardly watching them. Mrs Anscombe looked like Sarah in a way, with her thick black hair and wide mouth. Bel began quietly to clear away the toy animals.

"I've brought something for you, Sarah," the woman said. "It's out in the car. I'll get it in a minute. Oh, Sarah, you have grown."

Then she became silent, and sat holding Sarah's hand and gazing round the room. She seemed to see Bel only as part of the furniture. Perhaps she mistook her for one of the Snowdrop House children. Her eyes stopped at the pile of plastic letters still heaped on the table, but she clearly did not connect them with Sarah. Sarah was watching her mother. Bel felt sorry for both of them. They seemed resigned to never being able to do more than hold hands. But Sarah's mother did her best. Every now and then she thought of something to say and said it hurriedly, as though there was no point in saying it so she would get it over quickly. "I got stuck in the traffic coming here. There was a diversion on the motorway." "I might be moving back to live in Bishopcross again. That would be nice, Sarah, wouldn't it?" "I love these pictures on the walls. Did your friends paint them?" Sarah just sat and watched her.

"I'd better be off, then, Sarah," Bel said eventually. "I'll just clear up my things."

Don't take the cars, said Sarah. Tell my mother I can keep them. She can put them in my locker for me.

Her mother kept hold of Sarah's hand, but pulled back, shocked by the awful noises that her poor little girl was making. She used to make those noises all the time, but it had seemed that she was growing out of it.

"The cars? No, I won't take them. Yes, upstairs, you can take them upstairs." Bel turned to Sarah's mother. "I gave her these cars. Can you make sure they get put somewhere where they'll be safe for her?"

"Oh, how kind of you," said Sarah's mother, as though waking up. "Yes, she has a locker upstairs. We'll take them up there later, shall we, Sarah?"

102

Bel began to pack up the plastic letters and the scraps of paper, and then hesitated. "Did you want to show your mother?" she asked quietly. She imagined a scene where Sarah spelt out 'Mummy, I love you', or 'Now I can say all the things I have ever wanted to say', although of course they did not have enough words to say anything much better than 'Bel pig'. But Sarah was tired. She was beginning to forget which word was which. Her head ached. Tears began to roll down her cheeks.

"All right," said Bel, and gathered the handfuls of letters quickly into their box. "I'll come and see you next week. Goodbye, then. Goodbye, Mrs Anscombe."

15 Bel and Claire

"It's the big trip next week," said Claire, as they walked back from Willowbank. They had both been in the pool with the children and their wet hair was freezing on the backs of their necks. "After today I'm not so sure that I'm looking forward to it. It was really tiring holding all of them in the right position so that they felt as though they were swimming, especially the ones that kept kicking."

"I didn't have anyone small enough to hold," said Bel, "except that little tiny Lina, and I could hold her in my arms, she's only been a couple of times and she's just getting used to it. I had David jumping off the side for ages, and then I had one of the big ones who could really swim, I just had to walk in front of him encouraging him. And then Nicole came and interrogated me about where I'd got my swimming costume. The straps kept falling down. I spent the whole time hitching them up again. I'll definitely wear my plain black one next week. When David landed on top of me and grabbed hold of me, I thought the whole thing would come off."

"Do you think next week will be good?" said Claire. "Will they let us go down the slides and things, or will we just be helping the kids to paddle?"

"I think they'll need us to look after the children," said Bel. "They've worked it out at one adult for every two children, and we count as adults. But at least we

104

can see what it's like. It's supposed to have waterfalls and jacuzzis and everything."

"Dad said he'd take us there one day if we think it's good. Paul's really jealous about me going in school time."

Bel said nothing.

"Have you given up coming over to Dad's?"

"No," said Bel. "You didn't ask me last Saturday."

"You used not to need me to ask you," said Claire. "Anyway, I knew you were going to see Sarah. Come over this Saturday. There's an exhibition of sculptures made out of kitchen rubbish at the modern art museum. Dad's going to take us. I've seen a photograph of one of the things. It's an armadillo made out of baked bean tins, and it's brilliant. And they sell delicious food at the café in the basement, Dad's sure to take us there afterwards. You will come, won't you?"

"I would like to," said Bel. "But I told Sarah I'd come again this weekend."

"You can see her on Sunday," said Claire. "Come on, you can't use up all your Saturdays on Sarah."

"Sunday's no good," said Bel. "You know my gran comes over, and it's all right leaving her and Mum on their own after lunch just to go and do homework, but she wouldn't think much of me going out while she was there."

"Huh!" said Claire, pretending to be offended, but perhaps feeling really offended as well. "You take more care of your gran's feelings than you do of mine."

"Of course I do," said Bel quickly, trying to keep the conversation jokey. "She's ninety times older than you, and she's going to leave me her toby jug when she dies."

"Well, go on Saturday morning," said Claire.

"I'll try," said Bel. She wondered when her homework would get done, but she dared not offend Claire. "You don't fancy coming with me, do you? I said I'd try and take her to the station, but I don't really know if I can manage it on my own."

"Why on earth the station?"

"Well, you know one of the big classes went last week, and in assembly they showed their pictures of trains, and the tickets and everything, and Sarah said on Saturday that *she* never got to go to the station. She's never been on a train."

Bel saw Claire's face. Not just unbelieving, but pitying at Bel making up such a story. Bel wanted to feel angry, but more strongly she wanted to stay friends with Claire.

"Anyway, I thought it would be nice to take her. My father used to take us when we were little – you know there's that old turntable down by the canal; we used to walk along the canal from the meadow and then go up on the bridge and watch the trains. Of course I can't take Sarah down to the canal, but the station must be quite easy for wheelchairs. It has to be smooth for the luggage trolleys, doesn't it?"

"I'm not sure," said Claire. "I know when the station was new there was some fuss about it not being good for disabled people. Maybe you should go and check it out before you set out with Sarah. How will you get her there, anyway?"

"I suppose I could get her on to a bus," said Bel. "I can carry her a short way. She's not very heavy."

"But you can't just prop her up on the bus seat while you fetch in the buggy and pay for the ticket, can you?" said Claire. "She's too floppy. If nobody offers to help you, you'll be stuck."

Bel waited to see whether Claire would offer to help her.

"I'll come with you to check it out," said Claire.

"Thanks!" said Bel.

"But I'm not lugging her on and off buses. I think it's a waste of time."

"How about this afternoon after school?" said Bel.

"Piano lesson," said Claire. "Tomorrow?"

"Straight from school tomorrow," said Bel. "Thanks, Claire."

Bel decided that in a way it was nicer of Claire to come with her, seeing that she thought it was a waste of time. But perhaps she just fancied a trip to the station, and thought that Bel would buy her a bun at the cafeteria. Bel put the thought behind her, but reminded herself to take enough money for buns for both of them.

They caught a bus down to the town centre, and then walked to the station. Passing the ranks of taxis they came to the front entrance. The doors opened automatically, and the floor inside was on the same level as the pavement outside.

"See?" said Bel. "It'll be easy."

"Once you get her here," said Claire.

They wandered around in the strange plastic building. "What do you want to show her here, anyway?" said Claire.

"Well, the tickets first of all, I suppose," said Bel. "That's the first part of a journey, isn't it? I suppose we get platform tickets."

But there did not seem to be anywhere to buy platform tickets, and no-one was collecting or punching tickets at the doors on to the platform. "We'll just have to watch other people buying tickets," said Bel. "And I'll show her all the people carrying suitcases and things. And then we'll go out and see the trains."

Claire looked bored.

"Oh, Claire," said Bel. "Don't you feel excited at stations. It's like when I went to see Gran off to Canada at Heathrow. I wanted to jump on a plane and go flying round the world. When I hear that loudspeaker voice mumbling away about the next train on platform three, I feel like the beginning of a holiday."

Claire looked doubtful.

"Anyway, I want Sarah to see what people do when they go on a train journey, and to see a real train close up. In pictures they look so small, little caterpillars creeping through the countryside, and if Sarah's seen them at all, it's been from a distance. I want her to see how big and noisy they are."

"She'll probably be terrified."

"She might be, mightn't she? I'll try and warn her. Let's see where's going to be the best place to watch them."

A train was just pulling in to Platform One. People leaned out of windows to turn the door handles, and travellers on the platform dragged their luggage to the place where they thought the doors would stop. Porters hurried to and fro and a huge trolley full of mail bags was trundled up to the last carriage. "See, there's loads to look at!" said Bel. The porters began to blow their whistles and the train began to move again. A woman half-opened a door, and a porter slammed it shut on her. "Can't get off now!" he shouted. "You'll have to get off at Ostbury!" By now the train had got up speed. The woman, looking out despairingly, vanished into the distance.

"You won't be able to take her on to Platform Two, anyway," said Claire. "Look how you have to get there." She pointed up at a huge bridge, like a square glass tube crossing the tracks. The way up was by a glass-walled staircase.

"There must be a way for disabled people to get across," said Bel. "They can't only catch trains from Platform One. I'm going to ask."

"What's the point?" said Claire. "You can see just as much from this side."

"There must be a subway with a slope or something," said Bel. "I want to know." She asked a porter. He looked around for the wheelchair.

"I haven't got a wheelchair with me now," said Bel. "I'm coming on Saturday with a friend in a wheelchair, and I wanted to know."

"Well, a porter will help you if you want," he said. "You go out of the station, bear right, follow the road under the bridge, and then up on the other side and on to Platform Two that way."

"Right out to the road?" said Bel. "It's miles."

"Only a few hundred yards," said the porter. "And as I said, a porter will help you and your friend, if you ask." He moved away.

"There isn't a slope," Bel told Claire. "Never mind, we'll watch all the trains on this side. And maybe I'll take her for a bun in the cafeteria afterwards. I'm really glad I came to check it out. It looks fine, so long as I can get her here all right. Do you fancy a bun now?"

"I wouldn't mind a drink," said Claire.

They had Danish pastries and coke. "I think she'll enjoy it," said Bel firmly.

"You should take up train-spotting," said Claire. "Or get yourself a model railway. Paul's got a train set that he was given. He's never played with it." Claire could not believe Bel really thought that Sarah would be interested in the trains. Bel had to remind herself that Sarah had asked to be shown the station.

"Even if she doesn't understand much, it will make a change for her. Like a giant mobile, when the train goes by. An outdoor multi-sensory room. Noise, and smells, and big things whizzing by. Any of the Willowbank children would enjoy it, even if they didn't understand about journeys and tickets."

"I suppose it's been easier for me, with the little one," said Claire thoughtfully. "They are so small that you feel that any of them just might turn out to be able to do anything at all. It's easier to feel hopeful. All of them are improving quite a lot in one way or another."

"Well, Mrs Hinksey's lot are improving too, most of them," said Bel. "David doesn't seem so jumpy as when I first met him, and I think Joe talks more often. But Sarah doesn't seem to get a chance to improve. There's no room for her to improve, because nobody has found anything at all that she can do."

Claire looked at her. "Some people just can't do anything," she said. "It's not anyone's fault."

There were two different Sarahs. Bel thought about both of them. There was the one who smiled at her, who really understood every word she said and who one day would find a way of answering. And there was the completely handicapped Sarah, who smiled too, but meaninglessly, who must be trained not to upset people by kicking or screaming, and who would never be a real person.

"How's little Kim?" she asked, and Claire was happy to tell her as they ate their buns.

"I'll see if Gilly will help me with her on the bus," said Bel, still making plans for Saturday and hoping that Claire might offer to come. "She might if Godfrey comes too. Otherwise I won't risk it. You're right, it's too complicated with the buggy and everything. I'll push her all the way. It will take a while but it won't be impossible."

"Will they be taking her to Water World next week?" Claire asked.

"I suppose so," said Bel. "I think they're taking the whole school. The pool's closed to the public, so there's room for everyone. The Friends of Willowbank School are paying for lunch at the poolside café for all of them, and loads of parents and people are going to help. But don't tell Miss Radcot that, or she'll think they don't need us, and she was quite doubtful about

110

letting us go for the whole day anyway. We're missing all the boring lessons."

Suddenly a woman at the next table to theirs leapt to her feet. A train had just been announced. She swung her bag into the air and dashed off for the platform. The bag knocked Claire's drink over and coke poured into her lap. The woman shouted "Sorry!" over her shoulder and vanished through the automatic doors. Bel fetched a pile of paper serviettes from the counter and they dabbed Claire's trousers dry.

"Ugh, all sticky," said Claire. "I hate stations."

There was no chance of her helping on Saturday morning.

16   The Station

On Saturday afternoon, Sarah was put to bed for a
rest. She was certainly tired. It had been an extra-
ordinary morning. She couldn't wait to tell Duncan
about it. Duncan was always telling Sarah about the
places he had been to and the things he had seen.
Sarah did not think he had ever been to the station,
and she was sure he had never sat in the driver's cab
on a real train.

Bel had arrived straight after breakfast with Godfrey and Gilly. She said that Gilly was her sister, but
Sarah was not sure who Godfrey was. They had come
to help on the bus. Terry made them take a blanket
to tuck round Sarah in the buggy, although it didn't
seem very cold. Bel said the spring had come, because
there were flowers coming up in the flowerbeds,
yellow and white ones. The white ones were snow-
drops. Sarah wasn't sure about the others.

They went to the bus stop. Sarah could not remember ever being on a bus before. Godfrey lifted her on
to the bus, and Bel folded the buggy. She didn't know
about the safety catch at the side, and the driver had
to wait while she worked it out. Gilly bought the
tickets, and she tucked Sarah's into her glove for her
to look after it herself. Sarah felt like singing and
shouting with excitement, but she kept her mouth
firmly shut, and just watched everything.

When they got off the bus there were people everywhere. Sarah recognised these shops. Mrs Eaton had

brought her into town to buy clothes, and they had been to Lewis's to see Father Christmas. It was terribly crowded. People's coats brushed against her face and every now and then the wheels bumped into someone's foot. The streets grew emptier as they got nearer to the station.

Sarah had listened carefully to everything that Bel told her about tickets and trains. She knew that there would be a lot of noise. She wasn't worried about that. She planned to watch out for the special television screens that flashed up train information, and see the mailbags and the porters' uniforms and the shiny rails.

They saw everything. On Platform Three a short local train was waiting for the light to change to yellow. The driver leant out of his window and spoke to Sarah. It was unusual for anyone to speak straight to her. "Want to come up and have a look in my cab?"

"Can she?" Bel asked.

The man opened his door, jumped down and hoisted Sarah up into his seat. "No steering wheel, see?" he said. "Not much at all, is there? What do you think this one does?" He pointed to a lever in the middle of the control panel.

Sarah reached for it. Bel grabbed for her arm, probably afraid that the train would take off at top speed with Sarah in the driver's seat and the driver hanging out of the door. "It's all right," the driver said. "You can push it if you want."

But Sarah could only bang it. The driver pushed it for her and it gave out a huge hoot. Bel and Gilly jumped. Sarah roared with laughter. The driver lifted her down, and waved to her as the train slowly pulled out of the station.

They saw people running with suitcases and leaping on and off trains. A little engine striped like a wasp chugged along and then shunted to and fro, crossing three sets of points before it was where its driver wanted it. "Let's go up on the bridge," said Godfrey. "There'll be a great view from up there."

"It's stairs," said Bel. "There's no slope."

"That's all right," Godfrey said. "I can carry her." He unstrapped Sarah and lugged her up the stairs. Bel bounced the buggy up the stairs behind her.

Godfrey dumped Sarah into the buggy and pushed her up close to the glass wall of the bridge. Just then a goods train came towards them on the tracks below. It passed right below them, its trucks nearly empty, just a few lumps of coal on the rims to show what they had carried. Sarah could see the trap-doors in the bottom of the trucks that would let the coal out. Godfrey turned her round so that she could see the lights changing, and watch the train rattle away on the other side of the bridge. Soon afterwards a train full of gravel came the other way.

"We'd better go soon," said Bel. "It will take ages getting back to Snowdrop House."

One more train please, said Sarah.

"Aren't you getting cold?" Gilly asked.

No, I'm boiling.

They waited for a fast train that raced under the bridge, and then two more passenger trains. "Come on," said Gilly. "We can't stay for ever. We'll come back another day."

"Shall we have a cup of tea?" Godfrey suggested.

Bel did not seem very keen on that idea. Sarah did not know that Bel had promised Claire that she would walk with her to her father's house at half-past one. Sarah did not want a cup of tea, but she hoped she would get something to eat or drink. Gilly bought biscuits and drinks. She got orange for Sarah. It was fizzy and made her cough, but she loved it.

The journey home was not so good, in a crowded bus and all of them feeling tired, but Sarah was

114

triumphant. She was sick after lunch and Lisa put her to bed. She remembered that she had forgotten to look for the mailbags. Otherwise she had seen everything. Life was certainly getting more exciting. The station today, and next week the Water World swimming pool that all the children had been talking about for weeks. Even Bel was excited about it, Sarah could tell. She dozed off, dreaming about swimming pools.

17 The Swimming Pool

But on Wednesday morning there was a shock for her.

"I've brought all their swimming costumes," Davina said to Mrs Hinksey, swinging the enormous bag that they always used for swimming trips. "And enough towels to go round. But we didn't know if you were taking all of them."

"Oh yes," said Mrs Hinksey. "All except Sarah. There are just one or two from different classes staying. Morag in Mr Butterfield's class is having too many fits at the moment, they've changed her medication, and we've got a couple with bad colds. Someone's supposed to be visiting Sarah today, some sort of health check, and anyway it wouldn't really be her cup of tea, all that excitement. I'm staying here, and one of the classroom assistants, and all the rest are going. You've brought your armbands, Duncan, have you? Well done!"

So Davina took Sarah's swimming things back with her to Snowdrop House. When Sarah realised what was happening, she roared her protest. She was roaring when Bel and Claire arrived. Bel rushed to her and took her hand to get her attention. Her eyes were screwed up tight.

"What's the matter, Sarah? What's happened?"

Sarah could not stop roaring, and Mrs Hinksey asked Bel shortly to leave her alone, and help get the other children to the toilet and then on to the coach. She said something to Mrs Wallace about how this showed that they had been right not to take Sarah with them.

The sound of Sarah's cries was still echoing through the empty school when Bel led the last two children out to the coach. Bel sat with Duncan, and Claire with her favourite little Kim. The children were bubbling with excitement, but Bel could only think about Sarah. She wondered why she had not come on the trip. Was that why she was crying?

Once they arrived at the swimming pool, Bel was far too busy to worry about Sarah. The children were shepherded to the changing rooms and everyone helped to get them changed. Usually the undressing and dressing was part of the exercise, and the children were encouraged to do as much as possible themselves, but today no-one wanted to miss a minute of the wonderful pool, and the adults stripped the children at top speed. Bel was horrified to peel the t-shirt off a plump Down's boy and find a thick white scar all down his chest. She tried to ignore it, but her eyes kept returning to it as she folded his clothes and helped him into his trunks.

"It's hard, isn't it?" said the teacher. "He's had open heart surgery. They have enough problems without anything extra, but several of them have bad hearts, and a lot of them have chest problems or deafness as well. It does seem unfair."

The boy seemed healthy enough. Bel had to clutch his hand and make him wait for the others to be ready.

"This is amazing," said Claire, when they came through the showers into the pool area. A huge ship loomed ahead of them, with cannons on board spraying out water. A slide came down from one porthole, curving down into the shallow babies' pool. Other small slides were arranged round the pool, with ladders or stairs leading up to them. Bel's little boy

117

dashed into the water and raced over to the ship. Bel spent the next quarter of an hour following him up the steps inside the ship and down the little slide. At last he was ready for a rest, and lay down in the warm shallow water and looked up at the white gauze cloud suspended overhead. Suddenly a fine sprinkle of warm water began to fall from the cloud. The little boy laughed and reached his hands up to towards the falling water. Another little child cried out, shocked, but then spread out her hands to catch it.

Bel had a chance to look round the pool. There were plants everywhere. She was not sure whether they were real or not. Surely the palm trees could not be, although it was certainly warm enough in here. Still sitting in the pool, Bel slid over to the far side where she could see round the ship to the rest of the Water World. There was a large pool beyond the ship, marked 'Deep Water', with waterfalls round the edge, bridges leading over rivers and a separate pool where round blue and green caves spouting water were the lower ends of the huge chutes leading down from the top of the building. One of them was transparent, and Bel could see water splashing down along its whole winding length. She longed to climb up and try sliding down. It might be scary being able to see through the tube to the pool below, but it would be exciting.

One of the children took her hand and pulled her up to her feet. She wanted to go up to the jacuzzi. Bel looked questioningly at the nearest teacher. The teacher smiled and nodded, and came with them, bringing a few more children. They sat in the warm bubbling water, laughing and letting their feet be floated to the surface by the rising bubbles.

The jacuzzi was higher than the other pools, with a waterfall splashing down from its edge. Bel looked round at the children, some calmly wallowing, others excitedly exploring, and remembered Sarah. It would be hard to get her on to the slides, and dangerous to let her get into that part of the pool where the current swept you off round the whirlpool, but she could enjoy the sprinkling cloud and the bubbling jacuzzi as much as anyone. Bel wished the beastly educational psychologist would hurry up and rescue Sarah from stupid Willowbank.

Then, seeing the teachers quietly helping the children to find their way to the slides, supporting children beginning to swim, or sitting quietly by the timid ones as they gradually felt their way into deeper water, she undid the thought. Willowbank was only stupid about Sarah. Or rather, it had made a mistake. Anyone could make mistakes, but it was terrible that this should be such a big one.

Claire floated by in the pool below, leading two small children in armbands. Bel waved at her.

Miss Wastie, the head, suggested that when the children got out, Bel and Claire should go and have a quick turn on the water slides. A few of the children had tried them, but only sitting on a mat with a teacher. Miss Wastie felt that the school should take responsibility for anything at all risky. Bel and Claire leapt from the baby pool and ran for the chutes. They snatched up mats and raced up the steep stairs.

"Any other time there would be queues and queues for these slides," said Claire. "This is fantastic."

"Which one are you going down?" Bel asked.

A man in the pool uniform of pineapple-patterned shorts and shirt sat looking bored by the gaping tops of the tubes. "The white one's the steepest," he said. "The blue one's easiest."

"We've only got the one turn," said Claire. "We'll have to do the white one."

"I can't!" said Bel. "You can see through it!"

"Come on," said Claire. "I will if you will."

"You go first," said Bel.

"But you will come down the same one?"

"All right."

Claire arranged her mat carefully and climbed gingerly on. She edged forward towards the mouth of the tube. "It's not slippy enough," she said, and suddenly disappeared down the chute. Bel put her mat down and sat on it.

"Wait!" said the man. He was watching the bottom of the tubes on a television screen. "All right!"

Bel eased herself forward and then felt herself going. Immediately the tube curved and she was thrown up to the side. The water was gushing along and she was swept down with it. The splashing water obscured her view of the pools below, but when the tube bent the other way and she slid right up the side, clinging to the edges of her mat, she could see the palm trees straight ahead of her. She was not sure which way up she was. Straight ahead the tube seemed to vanish. She gasped, and felt herself drop as the tube veered steeply down. A few more bends, and suddenly she fell with a splash into ordinary water. She went down, lost her mat, came up gasping and saw Claire beside her.

"God, that was awful!" she said, shaking her hair out of her eyes.

"Here's your mat," said Claire, handing it to her.

"I wish we could go up again," said Bel.

"We'd better go and help them get dressed," said Claire. "Don't worry, Dad said he'd bring us some time. Let's tell him we've got to come next week."

Only a few of the children were dressed. The teachers had wrapped them all in towels to keep warm and were frantically pulling socks up over clammy feet and tugging jerseys over heads. Bel and Claire joined in and by the time all the children were dressed felt that they had earned the burgers and chips that the

Friends of Willowbank were providing. Bel and Claire went off to dress in separate cubicles, and then helped to load the swimming bags into the coach while the children were taken up to the café.

The pool staff were determined to make it a thorough treat, and some of them were in fancy dress. There were balloons everywhere, and the children were all given paper hats to wear. The pool manager brought out a guitar and played all the songs that anyone could think of with any mention in them of water. The singing went on in the coach home, and Bel and Claire arrived back as tired as the children.

They helped lift the children down from the coach and return them to their classes. Some parents had arrived to take them home, but most would be going home in the school minibuses. Bel led a group of children back to their class. The office door was open, and inside was Sarah in her buggy, her head hanging heavily to one side, one arm uncomfortably dangling.

"Hello," said Bel, feeling guilty at having enjoyed herself so much, and forgotten Sarah.

They wouldn't let me go swimming, and Mrs Hinksey tried to get Mrs Eaton to come and fetch me home, but they were all out and I've been here all day. I fell asleep, and I haven't had any lunch.

"Yes," said Bel doubtfully. She had caught the word 'swimming', but nothing else.

"Lunch," said Claire quietly behind her. "I think she hasn't had any lunch."

Mrs Hinksey came out of her classroom. "Ah, you're all back! Did you have a good time?"

"It was great," said Bel. "They all really enjoyed it."

"Well, Sarah quietened down a bit after you had left," said Mrs Hinksey, "but she really wasn't fit to be at school. I rang Snowdrop House several times, but they must have been out. The poor child hasn't even had any lunch yet, she was asleep when we had ours. Poor old Sarah, are you hungry?" She went and straightened Sarah in the buggy, then pushed her off towards the kitchen.

"How did you know she hadn't had lunch?" Bel demanded.

"She said so!" said Claire. "Didn't you hear her? And she said something about going home. Didn't you hear?"

"I don't understand her very well," Bel mumbled.

Claire stared at her. "If you'd told me she could talk!" she said.

"She can't!" said Bel. "Nobody understands her!"

Suddenly things were upside down. There was now no question about Claire's believing that Sarah had a brain, but it was hard that Claire, without caring about Sarah at all, without having spent weeks racking her brains for ways of communicating with her, could suddenly know what she was saying. Bel knew she should feel relieved, but she was annoyed. Sarah was her child, not Claire's.

18 Willowbank School

Miss Radcot liked to keep the last Wednesday afternoon of the term free for what she called an Open Forum. The children could report on their community placements, and share their experiences. The previous Wednesday, when it was too late to have much influence on the way the children were carrying out their tasks, she always took her camera round, making a flying visit to each group of children and capturing forever their service to the community. She had only got as far as the playgroup when she found that half of one wall was still bare undercoat. Sean and his friends had been waiting for some special tin of paint that had been ordered and the painting had simply not been done. They could not leave the job unfinished, so Miss Radcot, borrowing an overall that was hanging behind the playgroup door and which luckily looked quite painty already, threw herself into the task and they produced a rather wild scene from Tom and Jerry without the turquoise that Sean had thought essential.

It was a shame that she never got to Willowbank with her camera, because the two classes which had had most to do with Claire and Bel were having a farewell party. Bel had brought a cake, and Claire had made a special balloon for each child, with their names and a picture drawn on which swelled up nicely when the balloons were inflated.

They played 'The farmer's in his den' and 'Poor

Jenny lies a-weeping', and a game which Bel had prepared where each child was given half of a picture and had to find the other half somewhere in the school hall. Bel had spent hours drawing plain bright pictures of cars, ducks, Christmas trees, anything that she knew would be familiar, and then cut them with a jagged line making sure that each half held a recognisable part of the whole picture. It was not a total success. Some of the children did not catch on to the idea and went round collecting all the half-pictures they could find. David insisted on holding his finished picture upside-down and saying that it was a food processor. The right way up it was meant to be a horse. Duncan could not resist helping the smaller children to find their halves and did not give them a chance to look for themselves. But on the whole it went well.

After tea Mrs Wallace played the piano for some singing. Bel sat with Sylvia and tried to get her to join in. The child on the other side was enthusiastically joining in with all the actions for the songs, and Bel put Sylvia's hands through the motions. As they came noisily to the end of a song where everyone had to leap to their feet, jump, turn round, clap hands and sit down again, Bel, triumphant at having persuaded Sylvia to do all the different things, looked across at Claire, who had had two of the little ones on her lap all afternoon. The little ones had gone, and Claire was sitting with Sarah on her lap. Sarah was leaning back, her head hanging sideways and her eyes looking straight into Claire's. A wide smile split her face. Claire was smiling back and saying something. Bel stopped breathing for a moment. They were having a conversation. Claire was having a conversation with Sarah.

Sylvia began to squirm on Bel's lap. Bel, her head hot and her hands cold, gently held Sylvia's arms and tried to switch her mind back to the song. It was Old Macdonald. She barked and mooed in Sylvia's ear and made her laugh. Sylvia relaxed again, and the child on Bel's other side leaned giggling against Bel's arm.

When the party was over they took the children to their classrooms to calm down before the end of the day. Mrs Hinksey got out the building bricks and the playdough and let the children do whatever they wanted. Bel had expected to feel sad this last afternoon. The Snowdrop House children she would see again, but that was only a few. She looked around the classroom and felt as though she had already gone. Already she did not belong here. There were tears at the back of her eyes and throat, but they were angry tears, nothing to do with saying goodbye to these children.

When it was time to get the children into their coats, Bel went over to Sarah, who was lying on the mat. "Bye, Sarah. See you on Saturday."

Sarah smiled. Bye, see you.

It wasn't Sarah's fault, but Bel could not smile at her. She waved solemnly, thanked Mrs Hinksey for letting her do her community project here, accepted Mrs Hinksey's thanks for her help, and went outside to wait for Claire.

Claire came out beaming and gasping, tears running down her face. "Look what they made me, Bel! Look!"

It was a large card made of folded-over sugar-paper, with a picture on it of each of the children in the babies' class. They had been drawn by the grown-ups, but coloured in by the children themselves.

Bel hardly looked at it. Claire had taken over the whole school. Mrs Hinksey's class had not liked her enough to give her a goodbye card, and on top of that, Claire, who had always said that Sarah was a complete cabbage with no brain, had suddenly made friends with her and could talk with her in a way that Bel had no hope of doing.

"Did your class give you anything?" Claire asked as they left Willowbank's playground.

Bel shook her head.

"Mrs Hinksey should have organised it. They were just as fond of you as my lot were of me. I'm glad we were allowed to stick to the one class most of the time, although it was interesting seeing the other children. It was good to get to know a few children properly. The party went really well, didn't you think? They liked your game with the pictures."

"It wasn't any good," said Bel. "They didn't understand what they were looking for."

"Yes, they did," said Claire. "Most of them. And the ones who didn't understand at first were really pleased when they did get two pieces that fitted together. Kim was carrying his pieces of dog around saying 'Woof! Woof!' He wouldn't put them down all afternoon."

It was nice of Claire, but Bel's feelings were not to be so easily soothed. She kept remembering the way Claire's eyes had met Sarah's, as though they really understood each other.

"Don't be so upset," said Claire. "You'll be seeing some of the children again, won't you? And it was Sarah who was your special one, wasn't it? You'll be carrying on seeing her."

She's your special one now, Bel wanted to say, but she said nothing.

"You were right about her," said Claire. "I'm sorry I was horrible about her before. I just thought the teacher must be right. But she obviously knows what's going on. It's weird that they didn't see it. I don't understand much of what she says, but it's quite clear that she's talking sense. It's awkward, isn't it, when you don't quite know what she's said? I didn't know how to answer. If you ask her to repeat it there isn't much chance that it'll be any clearer the second time, and if you just smile and nod politely it might be all wrong."

Bel's rage had quietened down. She could see now that it was useless to be angry with Claire. Claire had made a mistake about Sarah, and apologised. Now she was discussing in a friendly way the problems of communicating with Sarah which at any time in the last two months Bel would have been delighted to discuss. But Bel was jealous. Instead of what had seemed like righteous anger, it was just mean jealousy, the feeling she had had a hundred times before, when Gilly won a camera in a colouring competition, or was invited to go to the pantomime without Bel. It was a feeling you were supposed to keep quiet about. You should be pleased about Gilly's camera or Claire's friendship with Sarah, and hide your own feelings completely.

"I feel jealous of you," Bel said, too much spit coming into her mouth, it was such a dreadful thing to say. "You seem so close to Sarah all of a sudden, and you can understand her."

It couldn't have been such a dreadful thing. Claire didn't look shocked. "I suppose it's a bit easier for me to understand her because I've got a good ear. That's what Mr Garsington said when he put me in for German. Some people are just better at hearing what people are saying. But it doesn't mean that she likes me more. I think she saw that I was treating her as a person, and she responded to that. And I'm only treating her as a person because of you. Anyway, you needn't be jealous. She wanted to go and sit with you, but I said I thought you'd got enough to do, looking after Sylvia. Was that all right?"

"Yes," said Bel. "I'd have got into trouble with Mrs Hinksey if I hadn't concentrated on Sylvia."

They walked on silently a little way. Then Bel noticed that Claire was looking sideways at her. "Bel," Claire hesitated. "Maybe I shouldn't say this, after what you just said, but I was going to ask if you'd mind me coming to Snowdrop House with you on Saturdays. Just sometimes, maybe. You've got me interested now. But if you'd rather I didn't, that's all right."

Bel was not sure how she felt about it, but she knew the right answer. "No, it would be great if you came. What about your father?"

"Well, we could go in the mornings, if that's all right with you, or maybe we could even get Dad to take us on some trips that Sarah could come on as well." They walked the rest of the way thinking happily about parks and zoos where they could show Sarah all the things that she had been deprived of, and that only they had thought of showing her.

As they reached the school, Bel remembered that today was the day for telephoning the educational psychologist. It had had to wait until the community project was finished, but it need not wait any longer. She said goodbye to Claire and hurried home.

19   At Bel's

It was lucky for Sarah that the school psychologist
had moved to Kent and been replaced by someone
new. The new psychologist, Miss Gupta, started only
a fortnight before the end of the spring term. She
planned to spend her first two weeks reading up the
old files, and then begin real work with the new term.
It was hard to know where to start. The Willowbank
Special School file was not the first one she had read.
The children there would all have severe learning
difficulties, and testing them was hardly a priority.

Miss Gupta read the files from the ordinary schools
first. They were thin files, because only a few children
at these schools were ever tested or even interviewed.
There were difficult children, slow children, clever
children, children with special problems. As she read
she felt impatient to meet them, and to help their
teachers to devise new ways of helping them. She
made notes about the children that she wanted to
visit first.

Reaching the end of one of these files, Miss Gupta
came to the Willowbank file. She put it aside, then
picked it up and flipped through the pages. It was
thick. There were forty children at the school, and
each of them had been tested at least once a year.
Most of the tests were routine and the results predict-
able. There was a loose page in the file. Sarah
Anscombe. Age, address, date of first test. Untestable.
Miss Gupta turned the page over. There was nothing

on the back. There was no information about Sarah Anscombe at all.

The telephone rang.

"Hello? Educational Psychology. Hello, yes, this is Miss Gupta speaking."

"Oh, hello," said Bel. "Is it you that tests the children at Willowbank School?"

"Yes, I cover Willowbank School. How can I help you?"

"Well, it's a bit awkward," said Bel. "You see, I've got to know one of the children who goes to that school, and I think maybe that last time you tested her, maybe she wasn't really doing her best. I think she can do more than people think she can. I mean, I know you're really good at it, and I don't want to interfere or anything, except that I don't think it's fair on Sarah."

"Who is this speaking, please?"

"My name is Isabel Taphouse. I've been helping at the school this term, and on Saturdays I visit Sarah at home."

Miss Gupta looked at the empty sheet of paper in front of her and picked up a pen. "It's very strange that you should have telephoned just now," she said. "Is it Sarah Anscombe you are speaking about?"

"Yes, Sarah Anscombe. She's in Mrs Hinksey's class. Why is it strange?"

"I happened to be looking at her file when you rang. I'm new here, you see. I've been reading my predecessor's files. But coincidences happen more often than one expects."

"What does her file say?" asked Bel.

"I'm afraid the contents of the file are confidential," said Miss Gupta automatically, although there was nothing in Sarah's file to keep secret. "But I would be pleased to hear what you have to say."

"Well, she's not stupid," said Bel. "She can understand anything. She can even make jokes. If you can just find a way for her to talk to you, she can prove it. She can sort of tip her head back to say yes, and pull it away from you to say no, and she can point with her eyes. I showed her some words, and she could pick out the right ones to answer questions. Only I don't think she likes being tested very much. She doesn't like being asked the same things over again."

"Not very many people do like being tested," said Miss Gupta. "But if you are right about her, she will have to understand that she has to prove herself before she can be helped. Can she point with her hands at all?"

"Well, sort of with her whole arm," said Bel. "But it's very hard work for her, and it's not very exact. She can only choose between two things really, if she's pointing."

"It's possible that her intelligence has been underrated," said Miss Gupta. "Mistakes are easily made. I shall discuss this with her teacher as soon as I can."

"Oh no," said Bel quickly. "Please don't. At least, don't mention me. You see, the teacher thinks I just unsettle Sarah. She is sure that Sarah doesn't understand anything." There was an awkward silence.

"Is that so," said Miss Gupta. "Well, I'll see what I can do. Perhaps you could give me your name again, and let me know how I can contact you. Is this your home or your work number? Oh, a school student. I see. Well, thank you very much for the information. Goodbye."

Now there was a little more writing on Sarah's sheet of paper. Miss Gupta sat and looked at it. A schoolgirl thought that the child was intelligent. The teacher thought not. Miss Gupta clicked open her brief-case and filled it with stacks of picture cards and boxes of small toys, then rang the number of Willowbank Special School. But the school had closed for the day. The cleaners could hear the telephone ringing in the locked office, but there was nothing they could do about it.

Bel went into the living room. As soon as she had arrived home she had shut the hall door firmly and dialled the psychologist's number before she could start to feel nervous. Now she saw that Gilly was home already, sitting on the sofa with books unopened on her lap. Bel wondered where Godfrey was.

"All right?" Mum asked.

"Well, I told her."

"You spoke to the right person? The one that tests the children at Sarah's school?"

Gilly was watching television. She got up and turned up the volume.

"Yes," said Bel in lower voice. "It's a new one. I told her about Sarah, and she just said she would see about it. I think it was a waste of time."

Of course Bel wanted Sarah's intelligence to be recognised, but a small part of her at the same time almost wanted things to carry on as before, with her being the only person to understand and help Sarah, her only defence against the stupidity of teachers and psychologists.

"Is she going to tell you what she finds out?" Mum asked.

"She took my phone number," said Bel. "But she said it was confidential. Maybe she won't tell me anything."

"We'll find out somehow," said Mum. "Don't worry. Let's wait a bit and give her a chance to see the little girl. Poor kid. I suppose it's worse for her if she is intelligent, so she knows what she's missing."

"She does get angry quite often," said Bel. "Mum, how would someone get like that?"

"What is she, spastic, isn't she?" said Mum. "Well, you don't inherit that from your family, or catch it or anything. I expect her brain was damaged when she was born. My cousin was like that, he didn't get enough oxygen at birth, but it didn't affect him so badly. He just walked a bit strangely. He was able to go to normal school and everything." She went to look around the kitchen and see if it gave her any ideas for tea. Bel heard her opening and closing cupboards and sighing as she saw the emptiness of the fridge.

Gilly was frowning at the television, hardly aware of what was on the screen, but intent on not being drawn into any conversation.

"I've just remembered that cheese flan," Mum called cheerfully from the kitchen. "Shall I warm it up?"

Bel was about to say "No", when Gilly called back, "Might as well", so she said nothing and went to join Mum in the kitchen. "Godfrey?" she said under her breath.

Mum raised her eyebrows and shook her head. Gilly had said nothing, but it was the first time for weeks that she had come home without Godfrey.

"Be nice," said Mum. "Sorry, I know you would anyway."

Bel and Mum smiled at each other across the table and shrugged their shoulders when Gilly poked critically at the hot cheese flan.

"I dreamt that Sarah was all right last night," said Bel. "She just got up out of her buggy when she saw me coming, and walked towards me. And she was talking, too. She was saying terribly clever things, but I couldn't remember them when I woke up. It was so real."

"If you do get her to say things," said Mum, "she probably won't be clever, you know. She hasn't really had the opportunity to become terribly clever."

"I know," said Bel. "All I want is for her to be ordinary."

But she thought of Sarah as a chrysalis, from which anything might emerge. Mum was warning her about dull grey moths, but Bel was expecting a butterfly.

20 Willowbank School

Every year Willowbank School and Snowdrop House ran a joint Spring Fayre to raise money for equipment and outings. It was held at the school, so that the stalls could be set up in the hall if the weather were bad, but usually they were lucky, and managed to catch one of the first really summery weekends of the year. Mrs Hinksey's class were making pencil-holders out of toilet rolls. It was a good craft activity for them, and people would buy them out of kindness. Mrs Hinksey even kept her pencils in one of these holders, on principle. The holder had been made by a boy in her class years before. The boy was now grown up and spent his days pulling plastic washers apart and packing them into bags of a hundred, but the pencil-holder with its bright poster colour decorations still stood on Mrs Hinksey's desk.

Later on, when the other children had finished, Mrs Hinskey would make a pencil-holder on Sarah's behalf. She would stick it together and paint zigzags and flowers on it, and tell Sarah that she had made it. She was not cheating, or not deliberately. All the children needed some help, Sarah simply more than the others. Until then, Sarah lay on a mat by the glass doors. Rain drops were following each other persistently down the glass. She wondered why they slid down at different speeds. It wasn't always the biggest ones that went fastest. One drop would swallow up another, then be destroyed by a new lash of rain smashing into the window. The sky was grey. The playground was grey.

"You all right, Sarah?" Duncan asked. "Shall I get you something to look at?"

I wouldn't mind a book.

"I can't get a book. Mrs Hinksey doesn't let me get them off the shelf."

All right, I'll do without.

Sarah turned back to the window. Duncan was a good friend to her, but he couldn't help. If the rain didn't stop then Sarah would have to wear her waterproof cape on the way home. Why couldn't she have a proper mackintosh like Timothy's, and just wear a hat and scarf to keep her ears and neck dry? When she could write, or talk, or whatever Bel was going to arrange, that is what she could ask for. A yellow coat like the lifeboatmen wear at sea, and the sort of hat that has a gutter round it to send all the rain shooting off behind you. Then Davina would get wet, if she was pushing the buggy, and serve her right.

"Sarah! Sarah!" It was Duncan again, sounding excited. "Sarah, a visitor for you!"

Sarah tried to look round, but she was firmly wedged on her side facing away from the door. She would have to wait to be turned over. Mrs Hinksey took Sarah's shoulder and moved her on to her back. A strange woman was standing beside Mrs Hinksey, her head nearly on the ceiling as Sarah looked up at her. She had tight dark hair and neat clothes like a doctor. She was not wearing a white coat, but the case that she held in her hand was black. It could have syringes and medicines in it. Sarah watched her warily.

"Miss Gupta has come to see you today, Sarah," Mrs Hinksey was saying. "Let's get you up in your buggy and you can go into the office with her."

"Hello, Sarah," said Miss Gupta. She knelt down

136

next to her and touched her cheek with one cold finger. "I've come to talk to you, and see if you can show me how clever you are."

"Sarah is very clever," said Duncan. "Sarah knows everything."

"Duncan!" said Mrs Hinksey sharply. "I thought I asked you to clear up those scissors and find the paintbrushes."

Duncan bustled away, and Miss Gupta and Mrs Hinksey between them lugged Sarah to her feet and then into the buggy.

"I hope you will be a good girl for Miss Gupta," said Mrs Hinksey warningly.

Sarah watched the walls and ceilings move past. Miss Gupta seemed quite good at pushing smoothly round corners and through doorways. She did not bump Sarah at all. What was she? Maybe not a doctor.

"Here we are, Sarah. I expect you have been in the office before. I'm the educational psychologist. My name is Miss Gupta. My job is to find out what all the children in the school are able to do, and what they might be able to learn."

Miss Gupta looked at the little girl across the table. She was small for an eight-year-old. She had nice hair, thick and dark, but it was not very well cut. She had dark eyes, and she was watching her very seriously. Miss Gupta felt that there was nothing to lose in talking to children as though they were intelligent. If they were very retarded it would soon become obvious.

"Now listen, Sarah. First of all, if we are to have a talk, I need to know if you understand me. What can you do to show that you have understood me?"

Sarah pulled her head back as far as it would go, keeping her eyes on Miss Gupta.

"Good, Sarah. That is a very clear sign. Will you use that for 'yes'?"

137

Yes.

"Right. And what about 'no'? Do you like this wet weather?"

No.

"Well done, Sarah, those are two good clear signs. I dare say you can speak, too, but your teacher tells me that she can't understand you, and as I am not so very good at understanding either, we'll keep to simple things first of all. Now, I've been talking to a friend of yours, Isabel Taphouse. Do you know who I mean?"

Yes, yes.

"She says you can understand a lot. That's good. But you have to show me just how much you can understand. Will you try to show me?"

Yes.

"All right then, Sarah. I'll ask you some questions. Some of them may seem very easy. Perhaps you will think they are silly. But do your best to answer them. Later we can move on to more interesting things."

Yes, all right, just get on with it. Why did that other doctor ask those stupid questions like "What is your name?" and "Can you make me a tower with these bricks?" At least this doctor knows enough to ask questions that I can answer with a yes or no.

"Is your name Sarah?"

Yes.

"Is my name Mrs Hinksey?"

No.

"What is this building that we are in? Is it a shop?"

No.

"Is it a hospital?"

No.

"Is it a school?"

Yes.

Miss Gupta was writing down Sarah's answers. She usually found that a child who understood the questions thought them funny, and laughed, but Sarah's face was serious. She was too anxious to make the most of this interview to see anything funny in it.

"Do you teach here?"

No.

"Do you learn here?"

No.

"I'll ask you that one again, Sarah," said Miss Gupta, with her pencil waiting above the paper. "I'm not quite clear about your answer. Are you a pupil at this school?"

Yes.

"That's very good. Now I'll show you some pictures." She took out a loose-leaf folder and opened it at the first page. It was divided into quarters, and in each quarter was a line drawing. "There are four pictures here. I'm going to tell you a word, and I want you to tell me which picture is the right picture for that word. So, if I say 'ball', you will point to this picture, because this is the picture of the ball. Do you understand?"

Yes.

"I don't know how easy it is for you to point, Sarah. Can you point to the ball?"

Sarah flung her arm on to the book.

"It is hard, isn't it? Look here, I'll make it easier. We'll put the book in the middle of the table, and with my pen I'll make lines on the table, so that the whole table is in four quarters."

Sarah wondered what Mrs Hinksey would say when she saw the felt pen lines on the table. It was all right. Nobody could blame Sarah. Miss Gupta folded the cover behind, and put the open page exactly in the middle of the quartered table. She held it in place so that Sarah's arm would not sweep it off the table. "Now, to point to the ball picture, you only need to put your hand in that quarter of the table. It's easier to point to a big bit of table, isn't it?"

Sarah's hand landed in the right quarter. "Good. Now, just for practice, show me the ring. Yes. Show me the cow. Good. And the car. Right, this will work well." She turned over to the next page. The pictures were of a pen, a cup, a bird and a glove. "Which is the cup? Oh, yes, this is too easy for you. Let's turn over some more pages."

She flipped through the book until she found the page she wanted. Something switched on in the back of Sarah's mind. The pages of this book were familiar. She had seen them before. Had someone tried to test her before? She tried to remember. There was something very uncomfortable about the memory, something that she did not want to recall.

"Now, which picture shows 'empty'? Good. Let's try another. Which picture shows 'frightened'? Good. Which picture shows 'steep'?"

The words got harder. Sarah did not know them all, but Miss Gupta let her keep on trying. Her arm was tired. Her elbow, shoulder and neck were joined together in a huge heavy ache. Her hand began to land on the wrong quarter.

"I have tired you out," said Miss Gupta. "Sorry, Sarah. But you've done very well. This test shows that you understand a lot of words, as many as some children who are older than you. You know, there are a lot of children who have the same problems as you. They can understand perfectly well, but they find it harder to make other people understand them. I have a friend who works with children with this problem. I'll arrange for him to see you. I think he may be able to help you to make yourself understood. Some of the children that he works with have typewriters, and they can write down what they want to say."

I couldn't work a typewriter. I can't even point to a picture in a book.

"Some of them can't use the typewriter with their

140

hands, so they use a pointer attached to their head, or perhaps their foot, to work the typewriter. I know my friend will be glad to meet you and see if he can help you. His name is Mr Avery."

When Sarah had been wheeled back to the classroom she leant back in her buggy watching Duncan and Joe playing with the sand. The pencil-holders were lined up on the shelf behind Mrs Hinksey's chair. Sarah could recognise Joe's with its wavering lines, and Sylvia's must be the one that was glistening with red paint all over, but Mrs Hinksey and Mrs Wallace had helped so much with the others that they could have been done by anyone.

Sarah wondered whether Mr Avery would really help. She warned herself not to expect too much. Bel had seemed to promise that she would make her talk, and nothing had come of that. Sarah thought over Miss Gupta's test, and the sets of pictures that she had shown her. Suddenly, the old memory came clearly into her mind. An elderly man with glasses had shown her those pictures before. He had asked her, just as Miss Gupta had, which was the ball, and Sarah had not told him. Was it because in those days she could not use her arm to point? Possibly, but Sarah also remembered feeling angry, furiously angry with the man. Probably he had treated her as a baby. Had she refused to try? If so, was it her own fault that everyone thought she was stupid?

"No, Duncan," Joe was squealing. "Not in my house! Drive away! Drive away!"

Joe always made houses in the damp sand. Duncan always drove trucks into them and knocked them down. Today there were no trucks in the sand tray and he was driving plastic dinosaurs instead. Mrs Hinksey liked to put a variety of stimulating toys in the sand. It was not her fault that Joe and Duncan always played the same game with them.

If I prove that I can understand things, Sarah thought, will I have to go to a different school? The school where they have typewriters? I will miss Duncan. He isn't very clever, but he's not stupid like grown ups are. He understands enough to be my friend. I don't want to go somewhere new.

"Come along, Sarah," said Mrs Hinksey briskly. "You've had your little break. Let's see if you can do some work for me now."

She brought to the nearest table a board with five pies painted on it. Joe stood nearby, eyeing them hungrily from the corner of his eye. The pies were all the same except for their size. Sarah had seen the puzzle so many times before that she had thought of many different ways of describing the pies: small, minute, tiny, teeny-weeny and titchy, or enough, nearly enough, not enough, nowhere near enough, and not worth eating. She knew that however hard she tried she could not pick them out by the little cherry-coloured knob screwed into each pie, or put them back into their holes. It was no use trying.

Mrs Hinksey sighed. "Well, some people don't seem to appreciate a treat. I suppose you may as well lie on the mat until break-time."

Sarah collapsed on to the floor with relief. She thought about Miss Gupta. Would she come back into the classroom in a minute, and say to Mrs Hinksey, "Sarah has proved that she is very clever, and from now on you are not to treat her like a baby?" But break-time came and went with rain still pouring down outside, and nothing seemed to have changed.

21 Bel and Claire

After the third Saturday, Bel had given up ringing to check that Sarah was in when she wanted to visit. Sarah always seemed to be there, parked in her buggy, when she arrived. So it was a shock when Bel and Claire let themselves into Snowdrop House and were told by Duncan that Sarah had gone out.

"She's gone to see the house," he told them. "Sarah's house."

"Where's Lisa?" Bel asked him. "Or Terry?" Claire stood a little behind her, recognising the children milling around, but feeling shy with them. Terry came through a door with a child in his arms.

"Hello, Bel, I thought you might come. I wish you'd rung. Mrs Anscombe came to take Sarah out, but I couldn't let you know. They've gone to see the new house. You know her mother's moved back down to Bishopcross, and she's going to have Sarah to live with her again. Oh, didn't you know? Yes, as soon as she's settled into her new job and the house is done up and everything. It'll be great for Sarah, won't it? But I'm afraid they've gone out for the whole day. I am sorry."

Bel turned to Claire. "We were hoping to take her out for a walk," said Claire. "Do you think someone else would like to come instead? We thought we'd go up to Combe Park and feed the ducks." She shook a plastic bag that held half a broken-up loaf. Bel was wondering whether it would really be so great for

Sarah to move into her mother's new house. Her mother hardly seemed to know her. To be fair, Mrs Anscombe had not treated Sarah like a baby. But she hadn't seemed at ease with her, when Bel had seen them together. Did she even like Sarah? Bel stopped herself. Here she was, jealous again. Probably Mrs Anscombe had been too shy to talk to her daughter in front of Bel, and even if she wasn't good at talking to her, she would soon get better at it. Of course Sarah would be pleased to be going to live with her.

Bel really wanted to feel that she was the one person who was important to Sarah, but she knew that it wasn't true.

Duncan was hugging Terry round the waist. "Me, Terry. Let me go with them."

"Yes, it would be great if you could take Duncan. He'll be very good, won't you, Duncan? I should think one's enough, isn't it, or would you like to take Tim as well? He wouldn't be any problem for you."

They took Duncan and Timothy. They went on the bus, which was easy without a wheelchair. Duncan and Timothy bought their own tickets, and chose their seats, the front ones on the top deck. Bel and Claire pushed them on the swings, encouraged them on the climbing frames and caught them off the slides. They fed the ducks and played hide-and-seek among the bushes, and visited the canaries and rabbits in the cages next to the football pitch.

"We can always bring Sarah here another time," Claire said as the two boys crouched down, pushing blades of grass through the wire netting to the rabbits. "She'll like the birds and things, and did you notice that the roundabout has special places for wheelchairs to fit on to?"

"Oh, is that what they were?" said Bel. "I couldn't work it out. Of course, she wouldn't be able to sit on an ordinary roundabout without someone holding her on the seat. Would she be able to go on a swing?"

They gazed at the swings.

"She's miles too big for the baby swings," Claire said. "And I don't think you could hold her on your lap safely. She's so floppy, and big."

"But swinging is lovely," Bel protested, as though there must be some solution to the problem. "She can't just not know what swinging is like."

"We could swing her in a blanket," Claire suggested. "It's the same sort of feeling. Mum and Dad used to do it to me when I was little. Dad and I tried to swing Paul one day. We were having a picnic by the river, and he was lying on the blanket, and we picked up one end each and swung him, and he was furious."

"Was he counting leaves, and you interrupted him?"

"Almost. He was into weather last summer, and he was looking at the cloud formations. What about this little guinea pig, Duncan? Do you think it would like some grass too?"

"Poor Paul," said Bel.

"Poor?" said Claire. "He's a pain. Poor me, having him for a brother."

"No, but he'll never enjoy nice things like swinging. His brain gets in the way. Sarah's got problems, but at least if we swing her in a blanket she can feel what it's like being swung. And that's why it's interesting being with her. Her problems are solvable."

"All of them?" asked Claire.

"Well, enough to keep us busy. Paul isn't solvable, is he? I think he's harder to understand than Sarah."

"You didn't mind me offering to bring someone else here, did you?" said Claire in a low voice. "I just said it without thinking, but maybe you were only interested in bringing Sarah."

"I was," said Bel. "I wanted to show her everything.

But I'm glad we brought Tim and Duncan. I hadn't really realised how much they could notice things, and enjoy themselves. It hasn't been a waste of time at all. I do still wish we could have brought Sarah, but not because she's got more brain, only because she hasn't been shown so many things up till now. But I wouldn't mind bringing these two out somewhere again."

"Will you be going to visit Sarah next Saturday if she's not out with her mother?" Claire asked.

"It's the start of the holidays next weekend," said Bel. "But I suppose I'm not doing anything special. Yes, I probably will."

"I forgot it was the holidays!" said Claire. "I was supposed to be asking you ages ago. Dad's taking us to Wales for a long weekend, Friday to Monday, and do you want to come with us? Please come. Paul's bringing his horrible little friend Jerome who's even more of a know-all, if that's possible. Dad will ring your mum, but I was supposed to be finding out if you wanted to come first."

"Of course I want to come. Is it mountains?"

The boys tired of feeding the rabbits. They went for a last swing and wandered back to the bus stop, stopping on the way to buy a packet of crisps for each of them. Duncan held Bel's hand and talked about crisps and rabbits and swings and what lunch would probably be. She might have seen him as a poor substitute for Sarah, but he definitely thought that she was a friend.

Handing the boys back to Terry, she told him that she would not be coming the next weekend.

"You'll want to see Sarah before she goes," he said. "But she'll still be here the weekend after that. I don't know exactly when her mother's planning to have her. We'll have to get a date off her, because we've got a waiting list for the beds here."

146

Bel imagined a queue of children, lining up outside Snowdrop House with their suitcases.

"Don't think we're glad to get rid of her," said Terry, watching Bel's expression. "But she will be better off with her mother."

Bel decided that on the Saturday after her holiday with Claire, she would bake a cake. She and Sarah would have a goodbye celebration. She would bring the books that Sarah had enjoyed most, perhaps some balloons. If Claire came, they might go to Combe Park and take a picnic. It must be good that Sarah was going with her mother, and Bel would not be jealous, but at least she could leave Sarah with something good to remember. She vaguely imagined a party, with Duncan, Sylvia, all the children playing 'oranges and lemons' or 'mulberry bush'.

Wales put all thoughts of school, Snowdrop House or Sarah out of Bel's mind, and when she came home from Wales, her father was home. She had known he was due back for a month's break, but had almost forgotten.

"Good trip?" he asked, without taking his eyes off the television.

"Yes, thanks, it was great. How's work, Dad?"

"Lousy. What do you expect?"

"There's a letter for you here somewhere, Bel," said Mum. "Great big envelope, postmarked Bishopcross. One of those free offers you've sent off for, I expect."

"I haven't sent away for anything for ages," said Bel. She tore it open and pulled out a folder. Inside was a sheet of paper covered with poster-paint hand-prints, each labelled with the name of a child from Mrs Hinksey's class, and a large photograph of the Willowbank school hall filled with beaming children. In the middle of the crowd she recognised herself, one arm around Sylvia, smiling at the little boy next to her. She shook the envelope and a letter slid out.

"It's from Mrs Hinksey," she said. "Thank you for all your help. I hope you will remember us all as fondly as we will you. The children have been asking after you, and we hope to see you again some time. I have an apology to make to you. It seems that you were right about Sarah Anscombe, and that I was quite wrong. A new educational psychologist has been retesting all the children; by some remarkable means she has managed to communicate with Sarah and has found that her I.Q. is at least average, so your efforts to include her in all our activities were not wasted at all. She will be starting next term at a different school. So congratulations on your perspicacity and again many thanks for your help."

"What a nice letter," said Mum. "She sounds a very nice person. And what a lovely picture! Did you know she was taking it?"

"I never noticed a camera at all," said Bel. "I thought she was really mean not to organise a good-bye card or anything for me, when Claire got one from the babies' class. But of course she had to wait to get the picture printed."

"Let's see." Dad held out his hand for the photograph, and then again for the letter. "What's all this?"

"It was my school community project," said Bel. "Claire and me helped at this special school. I wasn't keen at first, but it was good. I go and visit some of the children on Saturdays."

"Handicapped?" said Dad, looking closely at the photograph. "My next-door neighbours had a little boy like that when we lived in Ostbury. Could have been that little fellow there. Dead spit of him. Nice little thing. I used to play football with him. Most of the kids wouldn't play with him."

Bel leaned over his shoulder. "Which one?" she asked. "That's Duncan! He's one of my special ones. We took him to Combe Park a couple of weeks ago.

Dad, you wouldn't come with us some time, would you? He hasn't got a father, at least not one who sees him any more, and he'd think it was amazing to have a real man to play football with." She was cheating; she thought that she and Claire were quite capable of playing football with Duncan and Tim, and if Duncan thought a real man would be better, he should be taught otherwise. But it had come to her suddenly as a way of pleasing her father.

Dad grunted. "Maybe. I'll see how busy I am."

Mum had taken the letter back from Dad. "And how nice of her to apologise," she said. "A lot of teachers wouldn't."

"I wonder if she's apologised to Sarah," said Bel.

"None of your business," said Mum. "Now get that rucksack into your room and sort out which clothes need washing. If you changed your clothes at all while you were away."

22 Snowdrop House

Sarah woke up early on her last morning. One of the babies was growling, waiting to be got up, but everyone else was still asleep. The teddy-bear mobile over Sylvia's bed twirled slowly round, crooked since Sylvia had leapt up and grabbed at it. Sarah looked at Duncan's peaceful face turned softly on its pillow. His knitted elephant was on the floor. As soon as he woke he would be looking for it. During the day he did not care about it, but while he was in bed he could not bear to be without it. Tim was stirring. Sarah watched him roll over and back again, push back the cover, sniff, screw up his eyes, shake his head and go back to sleep.

Jean had said that Sarah could see all her old friends as often as she liked. They could come to visit them in their new house, or Sarah could come here to Snowdrop House. But already Sarah could see that it would not happen often. Duncan was probably the person she liked best in the world, but he was like someone on a television screen. The film here at Snowdrop House would go on and on, episode after episode the same. Sylvia always dashing about, Mrs Eaton always looking tired and patient, Duncan always cheerful and talking too much. Sarah could feel that by the end of today she would not belong in this world any more. She was going to change. The life that she would have with Jean would take her away from these people, and from this familiar world of cornflakes for breakfast but eggs on Sundays, bathtime at a quarter past six and medication at seven. She did not know who she was going to change into, but it would be someone completely different.

Jean was her mother. She had practised saying 'Jean' to herself. Jean had asked whether she wanted to call her 'Mum' or 'Mummy' or 'Mother', but all these words had felt strange and unfamiliar to both of them, so they had settled on 'Jean'. In letters Jean had always signed herself 'Mummy', but neither of them felt happy with it. Jean had let Sarah choose the material for the curtains in her new bedroom and the colour of paint for the cupboard and the door.

She had tried to tell Jean about Mrs Churchill stealing the money, but Jean could not understand. She was as bad at it as Mrs Hinksey, but at least she knew that Sarah was trying to say something. "Never mind," she had said. "I'll get better at understanding. It'll keep. When you've got your new typewriter you can tell me everything."

Jean had asked Sarah why she had never tried to talk to her. "I know I'm hopeless at understanding, even now that I'm trying my hardest. But you never tried to talk to me. You never pointed to things, the way you do now. It's obvious now that you are thinking about things, but when I used to come and visit, you never gave me a clue."

It was too hard to explain. When Sarah had tried to talk, people complained about her awful noises. At least her mother never complained about her. Her visits were peaceful. Sarah had not wanted to spoil them by doing anything that would make her mother look worried or frightened. She couldn't remember ever having chosen just to sit and do nothing, but she supposed now that it had been a choice. Perhaps things could have been different if she had tried to talk to Jean. Well, it would have to wait for the typewriter.

Here came Mrs Eaton to get them up. She pulled the curtains back and the sun came in through one of the windows. It shone through the crystal hanging by Tim's bed and made a rainbow on the opposite wall.

"Timmy's rainbow's on today," said Duncan. "Look, Timmy, your rainbow's on."

Sarah watched them getting dressed. Duncan struggling with his socks, Mrs Eaton trying to keep Sylvia still enough to do her buttons.

"We've got to have you smart today, Sylvie. You're going home today, aren't you? Home for Easter! Are you going to have some Easter eggs, do you think?"

"Easter eggs!" said Tim enthusiastically. "Chocolate eggs!"

Mrs Eaton searched in a drawer for Sylvia's cardigan and Sylvia shot across to the window, then back to the door. Mrs Eaton fielded her. "Come on, then, Duncan, not done your socks yet! You'll be too late to have any breakfast! Oh, look, this one's back to front. Here, this way round now. Come on, Duncan! Cheer up! What's the matter?"

Duncan was looking very glum.

"Now, I'm taking Sylvia down to breakfast and then I'll be up again and I expect those socks on, Duncan. If it's Easter eggs you're worrying about, I daresay the Easter bunny will be coming here as well, so there's no need to be jealous of Sylvia."

"Don't want eggs," said Duncan, and his mouth began to wobble.

Mrs Eaton and Sylvia's footsteps echoed on the stairs.

Don't be sad, said Sarah.

"Don't go away," said Duncan.

I'll come back to visit.

"You're not the same any more," said Duncan. "You've got a mummy and a house and a new school."

"Oh," said Mrs Eaton, coming back into the bedroom. "So that's the problem, is it? Here, I'll help you with those socks. Now, Duncan, do you know what Terry told me? He might take you shopping this morning, after we've said goodbye to Sarah. Perhaps you'll buy some buns, will you? Aren't you a lucky boy?"

"Me?" said Tim.

"Not today, Tim," said Mrs Eaton. "You're going out with your brother, aren't you? Come on, Duncan, let's get you dressed. You want to be ready to go shopping, don't you?"

Sarah was the last to be got up and dressed. Mrs Eaton put her in her new blue track suit with purple stripes down the legs that Jean had bought for her, and her new white trainers with the luminous laces. Sarah felt like dancing.

After breakfast Sarah was parked in the hall with her luggage next to her. Jean had brought in a suitcase for her things, and there was a carrier with her toys in it, the musical box and some teddies. She had given Bel's cars to Duncan. Sarah waited. Sylvia's parents came to fetch her. They waved to Sarah. A man came to fix one of the cookers that had gone wrong. Mrs Eaton went up to her flat, but came to the top of the stairs several times to see whether Sarah was still there.

At last there was a noise in the drive. A car pulled up outside.

"That might be her now," said Terry, opening the front door. "Hello, Mrs Anscombe. Come on in, she's all ready."

Suddenly Mrs Eaton was in the hall, and so was Lisa. Even Davina was there, although it was her day off. Children gathered.

I've been waiting since five this morning. Hurry up, Jean.

"Did you want to go straight off?" said Jean, looking vaguely round the hall. "No-one you need to say goodbye to?"

"Would you like a cup of tea, Mrs Anscombe?" Terry offered. He must have noticed that Jean seemed to think that it was too sudden just to take Sarah and go. "Oh, my goodness! I've just remembered that it's Saturday!"

"Come on, Terry," said Lisa. "You wouldn't be here if it wasn't Saturday."

Terry held his hand to his head. "Isabel comes on Saturdays, doesn't she. And I told her that Sarah would still be here today. That was before the date was fixed."

"She probably won't come," said Lisa. "She didn't turn up last week, did she?"

"Don't let us hold you up," Terry told Mrs Anscombe. "I mean, you're welcome to a cup of tea if you would like one?"

"Is this the Isabel I've heard about from Sarah's teacher?" Jean asked.

Of course it is. It's Bel! We can't go without saying goodbye to Bel!

"Bel! Oh yes, you call her Bel, don't you. I do want to meet her. I want to thank her. But there is a lot of sorting out to do at home. Well, Terry, perhaps we could have a cup of tea, but after that we'll have to go, Sarah. We can always find out Isabel's address and write to her, can't we?"

Everyone went into the dining room, where the tables were already set for lunch. Terry went to make the tea. The children stood round Sarah watching her. She had turned into someone new, an outsider.

Suddenly there was a noise in the hall.

That's her!

Duncan ran out into the hall. "It is!" he shouted. "It is Bel! And my other friend! Come in the dining room,

154

Bel." He dragged Bel and Claire in and brought them over to Sarah.

I'm going home today.

"Home?" said Claire. "Is it today you're going! Bel, you said she would still be here!"

I am still here.

"I'm sorry, Isabel," Terry said, coming through from the kitchen with a tray of mugs and a teapot. "I only just remembered that I'd told you Sarah wouldn't be leaving this soon. But I suppose I couldn't have rung you anyway. I don't have your number. It's lucky that Mrs Anscombe stayed long enough to catch you."

"I'm a bit late," said Bel. "I made this goodbye cake, and it just wouldn't cook. I kept looking in at it to see if it was done. That's why it's gone down in the middle. It's still a bit hot, I'm afraid." She took the cake tin out of her bag, pushing back the books and toys that she had brought for Sarah to play with for the last time. The children came nearer.

"A knife and some plates, I think," said Terry. He went to fetch them.

"Straight after breakfast!" said Mrs Eaton. "I don't know!"

"It looks a lovely cake," said Mrs Anscombe. "Isabel, I'm so glad to meet you. I heard that it was you who arranged for the psychologist to see Sarah."

"Well, it was a new psychologist," said Bel. "I expect she would have tested her sooner or later anyway."

"She might not have known what to look for," said Mrs Anscombe. "Look at all the people who never noticed what Sarah was trying to say. It seems so obvious now, when she says 'yes' or 'no'. But I really hadn't a clue. You've got a stupid mother, haven't you, Sarah?"

Terry cut the cake. Bel fed Sarah. Duncan sat next to Claire, holding her hand while he ate his slice of cake with his free hand.

"I want to hear all about it," Mrs Anscombe went on. "But perhaps not now. I'll give you our address, Bel. Perhaps you could come and visit us?"

"Thanks," said Bel. "Shall I come and visit you, Sarah?"

Sarah pulled her head back. Everyone could come and visit her. She would feel like a queen receiving foreign princes at her court. People would come and knock on the new yellow front door. The telephone would ring. Letters would come through the letter-box, only for her or for Jean. And when they didn't want visitors, they would not bother to answer.

"Don't worry," said Terry. "She's ignoring all of us these days. She's had her head in the clouds since her mother told her the date for her moving in. Doesn't care a bit about leaving all of us, do you, Sarah?"

Sarah saw Duncan's hand tighten round Claire's, and felt sorry for him. I do care about leaving you, Duncan, she said. Don't forget me.

"Now we really had better be off," said Jean. "Unless you want a drink, do you, Sarah, before we go?"

No, I do not want a drink. I want to go home!

They all stood on the step to see her leave. As her mother lifted her into the car, Sarah saw them. Duncan leaning against Bel, Bel and Claire waving and smiling. Terry darting after one of the little ones, Jennifer watching stolidly at Mrs Eaton's side, Lisa coming with a baby in her arms and making the baby wave.

Then Jean started the car up and Snowdrop House disappeared.

Founding Editors: Anne and Ian Serraillier

Chinua Achebe Things Fall Apart
Douglas Adams The Hitchhiker's Guide to the Galaxy
Vivien Alcock The Cuckoo Sister; The Monster Garden; The
Trial of Anna Cotman; A Kind of Thief
Margaret Atwood The Handmaid's Tale
J G Ballard Empire of the Sun
Nina Bawden The Witch's Daughter; A Handful of Thieves;
Carrie's War; The Robbers; Devil by the Sea; Kept in the Dark;
The Finding; Keeping Henry; Humbug
E R Braithwaite To Sir, With Love
John Branfield The Day I Shot My Dad
F Hodgson Burnett The Secret Garden
Ray Bradbury The Golden Apples of the Sun; The Illustrated
Man
Betsy Byars The Midnight Fox; Goodbye, Chicken Little; The
Pinballs
Victor Canning The Runaways; Flight of the Grey Goose
Ann Coburn Welcome to the Real World
Hannah Cole Bring in the Spring
Jane Leslie Conly Racso and the Rats of NIMH
Robert Cormier We All Fall Down
Roald Dahl Danny, The Champion of the World; The Wonderful
Story of Henry Sugar; George's Marvellous Medicine; The BFG;
The Witches; Boy; Going Solo; Charlie and the Chocolate
Factory; Matilda
Anita Desai The Village by the Sea
Charles Dickens A Christmas Carol; Great Expectations
Peter Dickinson The Gift; Annerton Pit; Healer
Berlie Doherty Granny was a Buffer Girl
Gerald Durrell My Family and Other Animals
J M Falkner Moonfleet
Anne Fine The Granny Project
Anne Frank The Diary of Anne Frank
Leon Garfield Six Apprentices
Jamila Gavin The Wheel of Surya
Adele Geras Snapshots of Paradise

Graham Greene The Third Man and The Fallen Idol; Brighton Rock

Thomas Hardy The Withered Arm and Other Wessex Tales

Rosemary Harris Zed

L P Hartley The Go-Between

Ernest Hemingway The Old Man and the Sea; A Farewell to Arms

Nat Hentoff Does this School have Capital Punishment?

Nigel Hinton Getting Free; Buddy; Buddy's Song

Minfong Ho Rice Without Rain

Anne Holm I Am David

Janni Howker Badger on the Barge; Isaac Campion

Linda Hoy Your Friend Rebecca

Barbara Ireson (Editor) In a Class of Their Own

Jennifer Johnston Shadows on Our Skin

Toeckey Jones Go Well, Stay Well

James Joyce A Portrait of the Artist as a Young Man

Geraldine Kaye Comfort Herself; A Breath of Fresh Air

Clive King Me and My Million

Dick King-Smith The Sheep-Pig

Daniel Keyes Flowers for Algernon

Elizabeth Laird Red Sky in the Morning; Kiss the Dust

D H Lawrence The Fox and The Virgin and the Gypsy; Selected Tales

Harper Lee To Kill a Mockingbird

Julius Lester Basketball Game

Ursula Le Guin A Wizard of Earthsea

C Day Lewis The Otterbury Incident

David Line Run for Your Life; Screaming High

Joan Lingard Across the Barricades; Into Exile; The Clearance; The File on Fraulein Berg

Penelope Lively The Ghost of Thomas Kempe

Jack London The Call of the Wild; White Fang

Bernard Mac Laverty Cal; The Best of Bernard Mac Laverty

Margaret Mahy The Haunting; The Catalogue of The Universe

Jan Mark Do You Read Me? Eight Short Stories

James Vance Marshall Walkabout

Somerset Maugham The Kite and Other Stories

Michael Morpurgo Waiting for Anya; My Friend Walter; The War of Jenkins' Ear

How many have you read?